Judy B. Gilbert

CLEAR SPEECH

FROM THE START

Basic Pronunciation and Listening Comprehension in North American English

Student's Book

CAMBRIDGE
UNIVERSITY PRESS

PUBLISHED BY THE PRESS SYNDICATE OF THE UNIVERSITY OF CAMBRIDGE
The Pitt Building, Trumpington Street, Cambridge, United Kingdom

CAMBRIDGE UNIVERSITY PRESS
The Edinburgh Building, Cambridge CB2 2RU, UK
40 West 20th Street, New York, NY 10011–4211, USA
477 Williamstown Road, Port Melbourne, VIC 3207, Australia
Ruiz de Alarcón 13, 28014 Madrid, Spain
Dock House, The Waterfront, Cape Town 8001, South Africa

http://www.cambridge.org

Telephone numbers given in this book have been created for practice purposes only and
all reasonable care has been taken to avoid using numbers that are currently in use.
However, the publisher takes no responsibility for the inadvertent use of actual numbers.

First published 2001
2nd printing 2001

Printed in the United States of America

Typeface Sabon   *System* Quark XPress® [AH]

A catalog record for this book is available from the British Library

Library of Congress Cataloging in Publication data
Gilbert, Judy B. (Judy Bogen)
Clear speech from the start : basic pronunciation and listening comprehension in North
American English : student's book / Judy B. Gilbert
p. cm.
ISBN 0-521-63737-6 (pbk.)
1. English language – Textbooks for foreign speakers. 2. English
language – Spoken English – Problems, exercises, etc. 3. English
language – Pronunciation – Problems, exercises, etc. 4. Listening –
Problems, exercises, etc. I. Title.
PE1128.G518 2000
428.3'4 – dc21   00-063090

ISBN 0 521 63737 6 Student's Book   ISBN 0 521 63736 8 Audio Cassettes
ISBN 0 521 63735 X Teacher's Resource Book ISBN 0 521 79966 X Audio CDs

Book design, art direction, and layout services: Adventure House, NYC
All illustrations done by Adam Hurwitz, except pages 35, 36, and 38, which were done by Judy B. Gilbert;
photographs on pages 126 and 127 were done by Paper Crane Design, Berkeley, CA.

Audio production by Richard LePage and Associates. "Bright Road" by Russ Gilman from his CD,
Back to the Barrelhouse.

Dedicated to the memory of
D. L. Bolinger

Contents

Appendices

Acknowledgments

Thanks to the following people for their generous help:

The manuscript reviewers: Adam Brown, David Mendelsohn, Barbara Seidlhofer, and Ellen Shaw, for their insight into fundamental issues.

Advisors on both theoretical and practical aspects: William Acton, Janet Anderson-Hsieh, Jennifer Jenkins, Bryan Jenner, Helene Lecar, Bet Mesmer, Richard Suter, and Martha Szabados.

Field-testers: William Acton, Elcio C. Alves de Souza, Noelle Anderson, Valerie Benson, Holly Beyersmith, Anna Chien, Melissa Chou, Barbara Gasdick, Greta Gorsuch, Nancye Haworth, Nancy Hilty, Anita Jepson-Gilbert, Judi Keen, Arlene Kisner, Sandra Marttinen, Joel McKee, Hana Otavova, Susanne Sullivan, Rita Thorakos, Edie Uber, Nancy Verdugo, and Beth Zielinsky.

Special advisors: Nancy Hilty and Alice Stiebel.

Special graphics: Dorothy Cribbs, for developing the original widened vowel font; Ames Kanemoto, for making and photographing the tongue position models, and for developing the concept of shrinking letters for continuants; and Judith Alderman, for drawing the tongue positions from the back.

Editors: Jane Mairs, for helping me resolve many difficult conflicts between linguistic facts and pedagogical reality; and Jennifer Bixby, for helping to keep the various elements coherent.

Publisher: Cambridge University Press, for its dedication to excellence, which gives editors time to do their best work, and specifically thanks to Colin Hayes for his long commitment to the Press position as the leader in pronunciation texts.

Jerry Gilbert, for advice on graphics, and for 48 years of companionship.

Introduction

This book is designed to give beginning students immediate help with English pronunciation. It concentrates on teaching those elements of pronunciation that will make the biggest difference in students' ability to understand the speech of others and to make themselves understood. The book is also intended to help students make use of English spelling by learning how to spell words, how to ask about spelling, and how to decode common spelling patterns.

Because beginners have so much to learn, this book presents only those aspects of pronunciation that are most urgently needed, leaving other issues for later study. Important skills and concepts are presented through graphic images, whenever possible, and recycled throughout the course in topic strands. These topic strands include the following:

- **The alphabet**: Using English letters to spell out loud in order to repair misunderstandings quickly.

- **Decoding spelling**: Using simple and efficient spelling rules to guess how a word is pronounced. Armed with these rules, students can use their books to practice what they learn in class.

- **Important sound contrasts**: Focusing on the presence or absence of the sounds that matter the most. These are the sounds that carry important grammatical meaning, such as the final -d that marks the past tense (as in "paid"), the final -s that indicates plural (as in "books"), and the final -s that marks verbs as third-person singular (as in "talks").

- **Syllable number**: Developing a greater awareness of syllables, and overcoming the tendency to add or drop syllables and thereby obscure meaning. Learners often leave out small words like "the" or word endings like "-ing" because they do not have a strong sense of the number of syllables in a word or sentence.

- **Strong and weak syllables (stressed and de-stressed)**: Lengthening vowels in stressed or strong syllables and shortening vowels in de-stressed or weak syllables. Because stress is so important in English, and is often used to focus attention on key words in a sentence, this kind of rhythm training can make a major difference in intelligibility.

- **Linking**: Linking words together. Students often have difficulty figuring out where a word ends and another one begins because of the English pattern of linking wherever possible. Practice with linking can help their listening comprehension.

- **The Music of English**: Learning the intonation and rhythm of English through communicative practice with sentences that are especially useful for beginners, such as:

  - How do you spell "time"?
  - What does "paid" mean?
  - What's that called? What's it for?
  - How do you pronounce L - E - S - S?
  - Did you say "cold"? No, I said "coal."
  - Where is it? What is it?

Letter to the Teacher

For years, teachers have been asking me to write a version of my intermediate-level book, *Clear Speech*, that would be usable for beginners. They said that it would make more sense to help students with pronunciation early, rather than wait until they have developed habits that are hard to overcome. Also, teachers often found that their beginning students became discouraged when people didn't understand what they were saying, and of course, a discouraged student is harder to teach. Teachers who were trying to help their beginning students with pronunciation expressed frustration with the limited results they were getting from traditional methods of drilling minimal pairs (e.g., ship/sheep) or asking students to "sound out" the letters in print. They were asking for a more effective approach.

All of this made sense to me. But the problem was that I just couldn't think of an approach that would work. For one thing, beginners simply don't have enough vocabulary to understand explanations. And with so much else to learn, there isn't much class time for pronunciation. One thing was clear to me: A really useful book had to be radically different from any other in the field, including my own intermediate-level book.

Over time, through much research and discussion, I developed a list of the essential elements of a pronunciation book for beginning students. These six essential elements are listed below. This list describes my approach to teaching beginning pronunciation and the approach taken in this text.

1 Concepts are taught through visual images instead of through words.

Students with little vocabulary have trouble processing written or spoken explanation. Therefore, I have used visuals as much as possible. For example:

- Extra-wide letters are used to show that strong (stressed) vowels last longer.

  ban **a** na

- Diminishing letters are used to show how a continuant sound continues.

  busss   belll

- "Music of English" boxes teach melody and rhythm in common phrases using pitch lines and extra-wide letters.

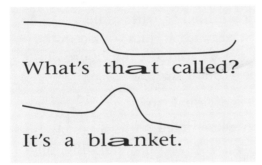

- Drawings and even photographs are used to show the tongue position for different sounds. In addition to showing views of the mouth from the side and from the top, a new perspective has been added: looking toward the front of the mouth, the way most people actually visualize their tongues.

2 Only the most crucial sounds are presented, leaving the rest for later study.

Because beginning students have so much else to learn, it is practical to focus their attention only on the most important sounds. These are the sounds that act as grammar cues, such as the plural "s" and the past tense "d."

3 Every teaching point is designed not only to help intelligibility but also to improve listening comprehension.

The most fundamental aspects of English pronunciation are also essential to listening comprehension. Therefore, to maximize the benefit to students, all new topics are first introduced through listening tasks in which students learn to hear the crucial distinctions before they begin to produce them.

4 Rhythm is taught through the visual and kinesthetic modes.

Most language learners unconsciously transfer the rhythm of their first language to any new language, which can seriously hamper their ability to communicate. Because rhythm is so instinctual and so physical, this book teaches the rhythm of English through visual and kinesthetic activities. Students tap out syllables and use rubber bands to practice lengthening stressed syllables, and the Music of English boxes use extra-wide letters to draw students' attention to the rhythm patterns of English speech.

5 Immediate help with reading is provided by teaching simple spelling rules.

Beginning students need to learn how to pronounce words based on their spelling so that they can read English with some accuracy. This book presents a few very basic rules for decoding combinations of letters (spelling) so that students can figure out how a particular spelling might be pronounced.

6 Tasks emphasize phrases, not just individual words.

People learn pronunciation best in whole fixed phrases, like the lyrics of a song. Learning the whole phrase rather than individual words imprints the rhythm, melody, and linking of the phrase. Short "musical" phrases are graphically presented in the Music of English boxes, providing students with useful language.

The only way to assure that a book truly works in the classroom is to have many cycles of field-testing by teachers working in different countries, at different levels, with different kinds of students. Many teachers around the world participated in this process. I hope their efforts will make the book a pleasure for you to use.

Judy B. Gilbert

CLEAR
SPEECH
FROM THE START

1 The alphabet and vowels

Cake, please.

A The alphabet

Listen.

Aa Bb Cc Dd Ee Ff Gg Hh Ii Jj Kk Ll Mm Nn
Oo Pp Qq Rr Ss Tt Uu Vv Ww Xx Yy Zz

B Vowel letters

Listen.

A   E   I   O   U

C Do you hear A?

1 Listen. Mark Yes or No.

	Yes	No	
1.	✓		(cake)
2.		✓	(rice)
3.			
4.			
5.			
6.			

A

cake

2 Listen again.

D Do you hear E?

1 Listen. Mark Yes or No.

	Yes	No	
1.	✓		(tea)
2.			
3.			
4.			
5.			
6.			

E

tea

2 Listen again.

🎧 **E** _**Do you hear I?**_

1 Listen. Mark Yes or No.

	Yes	No
1.	....	....
2.	....	....
3.	....	....
4.	....	....
5.	....	....
6.	....	....

I

ice

2 Listen again.

🎧 **F** _**Do you hear O?**_

1 Listen. Mark Yes or No.

	Yes	No
1.	....	....
2.	....	....
3.	....	....
4.	....	....
5.	....	....
6.	....	....

O

cone

2 Listen again.

🎧 **G** _**Do you hear U?**_

1 Listen. Mark Yes or No.

	Yes	No
1.	....	....
2.	....	....
3.	....	....
4.	....	....
5.	....	....
6.	....	....

U

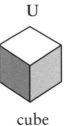

cube

2 Listen again.

Which word is different?

1 Listen to three words. One word is different. Mark it.

	X	Y	Z	
1.	....	....	✓	(see, see, say)
2.	....	....	....	
3.	....	....	....	
4.	....	....	....	
5.	....	....	....	
6.	....	....	....	
7.	....	....	....	
8.	....	....	....	

2 Listen again.

⌒ **I** **Saying the alphabet vowels**

Listen. Say each sound two times.

Letter	Sound
A	A^y
E	E^y
I	I^y

At the end of the sound
the lips are wide.

| O | O^w |
| U | U^w |

At the end of the sound
the lips are round.

J ***Key words for the alphabet vowels***

1 Listen. Say each key word two times.

Letter	Sound	Key word	
A	A^y	cake	
E	E^y	tea	
I	I^y	ice	
O	O^w	cone	
U	U^w	cube	

2 Write the key words.

Letter	Key word
A	....
E	....
I	....
O	....
U	....

K Food

Listen. Say each food two times.

FastBurger

MEALS	DESSERTS	BEVERAGES

• FastBurger
• Cheeseburger
• French fries
	• Ice cream cones
	  vanilla
	  chocolate
	• Pie
	• Cake
		• Coke
		• Milk
		• Lemonade
		• Coffee, Tea
		• Shakes
		  vanilla
		  chocolate

L Music of English ♫♪

Listen. Say each sentence two times.

Cake, please.

Tea, please.

The Two Vowel Rule

How do you spell "time"?

  A ___Saying the letters of the alphabet___

Listen. Say the names of the letters and the key words.

Letter	Key words for vowels
A	cake
B	
C	
D	
E	tea
F	
G	
H	
I	ice
J	
K	
L	
M	
N	
O	cone
P	
Q	
R	
S	
T	
U	cube
V	
W	
X	
Y	
Z	

B The Two Vowel Rule

1 Listen. Say each word two times.

2 Circle the first vowel letter in each word.

1. m@ke
2. rice
3. tea
4. pie
5. home
6. cube
7. soap
8. use

3 Read this rule.

> ### The Two Vowel Rule
>
> When there are two vowel letters in a word:
>
> 1. The first vowel says its alphabet name.
> 2. The second vowel is silent.
>
> This rule is true for many words.
>
> cake   tea   ice   cone   cube

C Words that end in the vowel letter -e

Listen. Say each word two times.

A^y	E^y	I^y	O^w	U^w
cake	Pete	ice	Coke	use
bake	see	rice	cone	cube
make	three	time	those	June
came	these	nine	home	rule
same	please	like	nose	cute

Words with two vowel letters together

Listen. Say each word two times.

A^y	E^y	I^y	O^w	U^w
rain	eat	pie	boat	cue
train	meat	tie	Joe	suit
paid	read	fries	soap	fruit
wait	see	cries	coat	

E **_Which vowel letter says its name?_**

1 For each word, circle the vowel letter that says its name.

1. m(a)de   paid   name   change   cake   Jane   Jake
2. cream   please   see   cheese   three   Pete
3. time   size   rice   like   write   bike   Mike
4. Coke   cone   boat   smoke   Joe
5. cute   cube   true   fruit   Sue

2 Check your answers with the class.

🎧 **F** **_Which vowel sound is it?_**

1 Listen. Say each word two times.

meat	meal	came	made	mine
see	soap	close	cue	cute
like	cheese	mile	rain	boat

2 Write each word in the correct box.

A^y cake	E^y tea	I^y ice	O^w cone	U^w cube
made	_meat_	_mine_		

3 Listen again.

G Music of English ♪♫♪

Listen. Say each sentence two times.

> How do you spell "time"?
>
> T - I - M - E.

H Pair work: Asking how to spell words

1 Listen.

2 Say the conversations with a partner.

Student A: How do you spell "same"?
Student B: S - A - M - E.
Student A: Right.

Student B: How do you spell "cone"?
Student A: C - A - N - E.
Student B: No, it's C - O - N - E.

I Pair work: How do you spell "cheese"?

1 Student A, ask how to spell a word from the Words box on the next page.

2 Student B, spell the word.

3 Take turns asking questions.

Examples

Student A: How do you spell "cheese"?
Student B: C - H - E - E - S - E.
Student A: Right.

cheese

Student B: How do you spell "tree"?
Student A: T - E - A.
Student B: No, it's T - R - E - E.

Words

sale	same	take	cake	page
tea	tree	cheese	please	each
ice	size	rice	time	fries
close	hope	cone	coat	soap
cute	use	cube		

J *Spelling game* EXTRA

1 Divide into Team A and Team B.

2 Team A student, say the number and letter of a word from the box below.

3 Team B student, spell and pronounce the word.

4 Teams take turns asking questions.

5 Teams get one point for each correct answer.

Examples

Team A student: E-4
Team B student: S - H - A - K - E. Shake.

Team B student: B-3
Team A student: P - E - T - E. Pete.

	1	2	3	4	5
A	made	name	Mike	Jane	pie
B	please	sale	Pete	team	page
C	cute	cheese	June	write	each
D	change	ice	boat	time	fries
E	cake	rice	cone	shake	soap

3 Syllables

How many syllables are in "city"?

A Syllables ☐ ☐ ☐

1 A syllable is a small part of a word. Listen.

cake   burger   cheeseburger

☐   ☐ ☐   ☐ ☐ ☐

2 Listen to the syllables in these words.

shake   milkshake   banana   banana milkshake

☐   ☐ ☐   ☐ ☐ ☐   ☐ ☐ ☐ ☐ ☐

B Tapping the syllables ☐ ☐ ☐

Listen. Tap one time for each syllable.

☐	☐ ☐	☐ ☐ ☐	☐ ☐ ☐ ☐	☐ ☐ ☐ ☐ ☐
shake	chocolate	vanilla	chocolate milkshake	vanilla milkshake
Coke	ice cream	cheese sandwich	turkey sandwich	banana milkshake
tea	iced tea	tomato	banana pie	potato salad
cheese	burger	cucumber	baked potato	tomato salad
pie	salad	lemonade		

1 Listen to three words. One word is different. Mark it.

	X	Y	Z	
1.	....	....	✓	(sit, sit, city)
2.	....	....	....	
3.	....	....	....	
4.	....	....	....	
5.	....	....	....	
6.	....	....	....	
7.	....	....	....	
8.	....	....	....	
9.	....	....	....	
10.	....	....	....	

city

2 Listen again.

🎧 **D** ___Counting syllables___ ☐ ☐ ☐

1 Listen. Write the number of syllables you hear.

1.	2	(cola)
2.	....	
3.	....	
4.	....	
5.	....	
6.	....	
7.	....	
8.	....	
9.	....	
10.	....	

cola

2 Listen again.

E   *Pair work: One or two syllables?*   ☐ ☐ ☐

1 Student A, say word **a** or word **b**.

2 Student B, hold up one or two fingers.

3 Take turns saying the words below.

Examples

Student A: Ninety.
Student B: (Hold up two fingers.)

Student B: Eight.
Student A: (Hold up one finger.)

1. a. ninety
   b. nine

2. a. eighty
   b. eight

3. a. four
   b. forty

4. a. sixty
   b. six

5. a. rain
   b. raining

6. a. rented
   b. rent

7. a. store
   b. a store

8. a. sit
   b. city

9. a. blow
   b. below

10. a. cleaned
    b. clean it

F   *Tapping syllables in words*

1 Listen.

2 Cover the words. Listen again. Say each word and tap the syllables.

3 Write the number of syllables.

1. banana   1. ___3___
2. sandwich   2. _____
3. milkshake   3. _____
4. painted   4. _____
5. rented   5. _____
6. closed   6. _____
7. opened   7. _____
8. cleaned   8. _____

G *Tapping syllables in groups of words*

Listen. Say each group of words and tap the syllables.

1. a cheeseburger
2. a vanilla milkshake
3. a cheeseburger and fries
4. cheesecake and coffee
5. pie or ice cream
6. two salads and one milk

 H *Music of English*

Listen. Say each line two times.

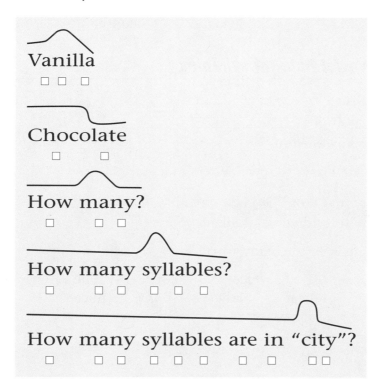

I Pair work: How many syllables are in "forty"? ☐ ☐ ☐

1 Student A, choose a word from the list below. Ask how many syllables are in the word.

2 Student B, hold up one, two, or three fingers.

3 Take turns asking questions.

Examples

Student A: How many syllables are in "forty"?
Student B: (Hold up two fingers.)

Student B: How many syllables are in "vanilla"?
Student A: (Hold up three fingers.)

city	a city	salad	burger	store
forty	computer	a class	forty pies	coffee
class	vanilla	milkshake	cucumber	ice cream cone

 ## J The Two Vowel Rule for syllables

1 Read the rule.

> **The Two Vowel Rule**
>
> When there are two vowel letters in a SYLLABLE:
>
> 1. The first vowel says its alphabet name.
> 2. The second vowel is silent.
>
> This rule is true for many words.
>
> | cake | tea | ice | cone | cube |
> | remain | repeat | arrive | soapy | juice |

2 Listen. Say each word two times.

A^y	E^y	I^y	O^w	U^w
rain	please	wife	road	true
explain	repeat	mine	soap	juice
remain	complete	arrive	soapy	excuse

K *Pair work: How do you spell "city"?*

1 Student A, ask question **a** or **b**.

2 Student B, answer.

3 Take turns asking questions.

Examples

Student A: How do you spell "sit"?
Student B: S - I - T.

Student B: How do you spell "forty"?
Student A: F - O - U - R.
Student B: No, it's F - O - R - T - Y.

1. a. How do you spell "city"?   C - I - T - Y.
   b. How do you spell "sit"?   S - I - T.

2. a. How do you spell "four"?   F - O - U - R.
   b. How do you spell "forty"?   F - O - R - T - Y.

3. a. How do you spell "raining"?   R - A - I - N - I - N - G.
   b. How do you spell "rain"?   R - A - I - N.

4. a. How do you spell "rent"?   R - E - N - T.
   b. How do you spell "rented"?   R - E - N - T - E - D.

5. a. How do you spell "six"?   S - I - X.
   b. How do you spell "sixty"?   S - I - X - T - Y.

6. a. How do you spell "store"?   S - T - O - R - E.
   b. How do you spell "a store"?   A S - T - O - R - E.

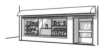

7. a. How do you spell "seventy"?   S - E - V - E - N - T - Y.
   b. How do you spell "seven"?   S - E - V - E - N.

8. a. How do you spell "soap"?   S - O - A - P.
   b. How do you spell "soapy"?   S - O - A - P - Y.

9. a. How do you spell "painted"?   P - A - I - N - T - E - D.
    b. How do you spell "paint"?   P - A - I - N - T.

10. a. How do you spell "salt"?   S - A - L - T.
     b. How do you spell "salad"?   S - A - L - A - D.

L   *Food game*   `EXTRA`

1 Divide into teams.

2 Each team thinks of food words and writes the words in the boxes.

3 After five minutes, compare your boxes. Each team gets one point for each syllable.

1 syllable ☐	2 syllables ☐☐	3 syllables ☐☐☐	4 syllables ☐☐☐☐
rice	ice cream	banana	macaroni

4 The One Vowel Rule
Linking with N

What does "less" mean?
How do you say L - E - A - S - E?

A The Green family and the Two Vowel Rule

1 This is a family tree. Listen to the names.

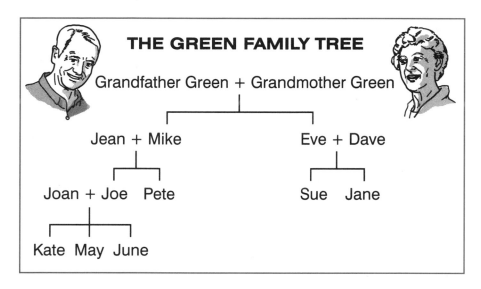

THE GREEN FAMILY TREE

Grandfather Green + Grandmother Green

Jean + Mike   Eve + Dave

Joan + Joe Pete   Sue   Jane

Kate May June

2 In the Green family, all the names follow the
Two Vowel Rule.

The Two Vowel Rule

When there are two vowel letters in a syllable:

1. The first vowel says its alphabet name.
2. The second vowel is silent.

This rule is true for many words.

remain	repeat	arrive	soapy	excuse
Jane	Jean	Mike	Joe	Sue

Pair work: Questions about the Green family

Ask each other questions about the Green family.
Write your answers.

1. Who is Joe's brother? ....Pete....................
2. Who is Jane's sister? ....
3. Who is Eve's mother? ....
4. Who is May's father? ....
5. Who is Grandmother Green's son? ....
6. Who are Kate's sisters? ....
7. Who is Dave's wife? ....
8. Who are Jean's sons? ....

C **The Red family and the One Vowel Rule**

1 This is the Red family. Listen.

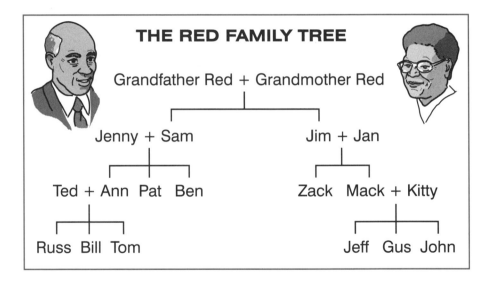

THE RED FAMILY TREE

Grandfather Red + Grandmother Red

Jenny + Sam   Jim + Jan

Ted + Ann Pat Ben   Zack   Mack + Kitty

Russ Bill Tom   Jeff Gus John

2 In the Red family, all the names follow the One Vowel Rule.

The One Vowel Rule

When there is only one vowel letter in a syllable:

1. The vowel letter does NOT say its alphabet name.
2. The vowel letter says its RELATIVE sound.

This rule is true for many words.

| can | pencil | finger | hot | summer |
| Mack | Jenny | Kitty | John | Russ |

D Words with relative vowel sounds

Listen.

A	E	I	O	U
Pat	Ben	Jim	Tom	Gus
hat	bed	his	hot	bus
Zack	pen	Bill	pot	sun
thanks	pencil	finish	John	sunny
Sam	Betty	Kitty	Johnny	supper

E Alphabet vowels and relative vowels

Alphabet vowels say their names. Relative vowels have a different sound.

1 These names have alphabet vowel sounds. Listen.

A^y	E^y	I^y	O^w	U^w
Jane	Jean	Mike	Joe	June

2 These names have relative vowel sounds. Listen.

A	E	I	O	U
Jan	Jen	Bill	Tom	Gus

F Which word is different?

1 Listen to three words. One word is different. Mark it.

	X	Y	Z	
1.	....	✓	....	(mate, mat, mate)
2.	....	....	....	
3.	....	....	....	
4.	....	....	....	
5.	....	....	....	
6.	....	....	....	
7.	....	....	....	

2 Listen again.

G Listening to vowel sounds

Listen. Point to each word as you hear it.

A^y A	E^y E	I^y I	O^w O	U^w U
Kate cat	teen ten	ice is	load lot	cute cut
Jane Jan	Jean Jen	file fill	Joan John	cube cub
ate at	meat met	time Tim	hope hop	rule run
same Sam	seat set	bite bit	coat cot	tube tub

H Which vowel sound do you hear?

1 Listen. Some words have alphabet vowel sounds and some have relative vowel sounds.

cute	teen	rule	ride	pine	lease
made	road	main	cube	ice	coast
hop	shake	less	mad	rod	man
cheese	fun	chess	cub	shack	ten
rid	cut	hot	is	hope	pin

2 Write the words in the correct boxes. Each box has three words.

A^y	E^y	I^y	O^w	U^w
made	cheese			cute
A	**E**	**I**	**O**	**U**
		rid	hop	

3 Check your answers with the class.

Listen. Say each sentence two times.

What does "less" mean?

How do you say L - E - A - S - E?

J *Pair work: How do you say L-E-S-S?*

1 Student A, ask question **a** or **b**.

2 Student B, answer the question.

3 Take turns asking questions.

Examples

Student A: What does "less" mean?
Student B: Not as much.

Student B: How do you say S - H - A - K - E?
Student A: Shake.

1. a. What does "lease" mean?   To rent, usually for a year.
   b. What does "less" mean?   Not as much.

2. a. How do you say
      S - H - A - C - K?   Shack.
   b. How do you say
      S - H - A - K - E?   Shake.

3. a. What does "shake" mean?   A drink made of
                                      ice cream.

   b. What does "shack" mean?   A very poor house.

4. a. How do you say
  L - E - A - S - E?   Lease.
  b. How do you say
  L - E - S - S?   Less.

5. a. How do you spell "wheel"?   W - H - E - E - L.
  b. How do you spell "well"?   W - E - L - L.

6. a. How do you say I - C - E?   Ice.
  b. How do you say I - S?   Is.

7. a. How do you spell "while"?   W - H - I - L - E.
  b. How do you spell "will"?   W - I - L - L.

8. a. What does "main" mean?   The most important.
  b. What does "man" mean?   A male person.

9. a. How do you say
  C - H - E - S - S?   Chess.
  b. How do you say
  C - H - E - E - S - E?   Cheese.

10. a. What does "made" mean?   The past of "make."
  b. What does "mad" mean?   Angry.

K *Linking with the sound N*

Many words are linked together.

1 The sound **N** links to a vowel sound at the beginning of the next word. Listen.

Dan is.   Dannnis .

an apple   annnapple

2 The sound **N** links to another **N** sound at the beginning of the next word. Listen.

John knows.   Johnnnknows .

ten names   tennnnames

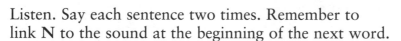

L   *More linking with N*

Listen. Say each sentence two times. Remember to
link **N** to the sound at the beginning of the next word.

1. Dan is here.   Dannnis here.
2. Ken asks questions.   Kennnasks questions.
3. Jan and I will go.   Jannnand I will go.
4. Joan always goes.   Joannnalways goes.
5. Jean never goes.   Jeannnnever goes.
6. John knows everything.   Johnnnknows everything.
7. This is an ice cube.   This is annnice cube.
8. I want an apple.   I want annnapple .
9. The list has ten names.   The list has tennnnames .
10. Have you seen Nancy?   Have you seennnNancy ?

M   *Review: Names of the alphabet letters*

Say the names of the letters in each group. The letter names in
each group have the same vowel sound. Read down.

A^y cake	E^y tea	E ten	I^y ice	O^w cone	U^w cube
A	B	F	I	O	U
H	C	L	Y		Q
J	D	M			W
K	E	N			
	G	S			
	P	X			
	T				
	V				
	Z				

R does not belong in any of these groups. It is pronounced
like the word "are."

5 Strong syllables
Linking with M

What's that called?
What's it for?

A Strong syllables

1 Listen.

   1. Canada

      Ca nada

   2. America

      Am e rica

   3. Australia

      Austra lia

   4. Cambodia

      Camb o dia

2 Read this rule.

> **The Strong Syllable Rule**
>
> When you say a word alone:
>
>   1. Each word has one strong syllable.
>   2. The vowel in a strong syllable is long.
>
>   pa per   pe ncil   compu ter

3 Listen. Say this word two times.

ba na na

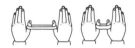 **B** ___Listening for strong syllables___

1 Listen for the strong syllable in each word. Circle the long vowel in the strong syllable.

1. ban(a)na   5. vanilla
2. Canada   6. chocolate
3. freezer   7. elephant
4. blanket   8. America

2 Check your answers with the class.

 **C** ___Saying strong syllables___

Listen. Say each word two times. In the strong syllable, make the vowel long.

1. sofa

so fa

2. blanket

bl**a**nket

3. carpet

c**a**rpet

4. newspaper

n**e**wspaper

5. telephone

t**e**lephone

6. washing machine

w**a**shing machine

7. refrigerator

refr**i**gerator

8. television

t**e**levision

9. freezer

fr**ee**zer

10. alarm clock

al**a**rm clock

11. can opener

c**a**n opener

12. vacuum cleaner

v**a**cuum cleaner

13. ceiling

c**e**iling

14. bathtub

b**a**thtub

D *Strong syllables in sentences*

1 Review this rule.

The Strong Syllable Rule

When you say a word alone:

1. Each word has one strong syllable.
2. The vowel in a strong syllable is long.

p**a**per   p**e**ncil   comp**u**ter

---

2 Read this new rule.

Another Strong Syllable Rule

When you say words in a SENTENCE:

1. One word is the most important.
2. The vowel in the strong syllable of the important word is extra long.

I need a p**e**ncil .   I n**ee**ded a pencil.

🎧 **E**   *Music of English* 🎵♪

Listen. Say each sentence two times.

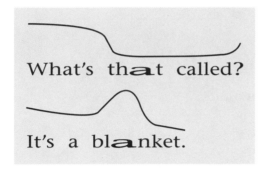

What's th**a**t called?

It's a bl**a**nket.

F   *Pair work: What's that called?*

1 Student A, point to a picture on the next page and ask, "What's that called?"

2 Student B, say an answer from the Answers box.

3 Take turns asking questions.

Examples

Student A: (Point to picture of a blanket.) What's th**a**t called?
Student B: It's a bl**a**nket .

Student B: (Point to picture of a telephone.) What's th**a**t called?
Student A: It's a t**e**lephone .

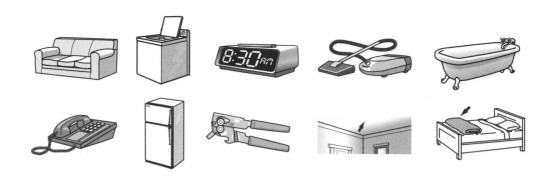

Answers

It's a telephone.	It's a can opener.
It's a sofa.	It's a blanket.
It's a washing machine.	It's an alarm clock.
It's a refrigerator.	It's a ceiling.
It's a vacuum cleaner.	It's a bathtub.

G Music of English 🎵🎵

Listen. Say each sentence two times.

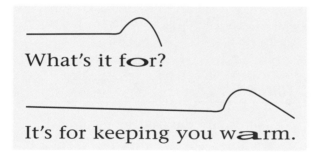

What's it f**o**r?

It's for keeping you w**a**rm.

H What's it for?

Listen. Say each sentence two times.

1. It's for **ca**lling people.
2. It's for keeping food **cold** .
3. It's for waking you **up** .
4. It's for opening **cans** .
5. It's for watching **shows** .
6. It's for reading the **news** .
7. It's for **si**tting on.

8. It's for cleaning the carpet .

9. It's for keeping you warm .

10. It's for washing clothes .

I Pair work: What's it for?

1 Student A, say a word from the Words box below.
Ask, "What's it for?"

2 Student B, say an answer from the list in H on pages 30 and 31.

3 Take turns asking questions.

Examples

Student A: Television . What's it for ?
Student B: It's for watching shows .

Student B: Newspaper . What's it for ?
Student A: It's for reading the news .

Words

television	telephone	refrigerator	newspaper
blanket	sofa	can opener	alarm clock
washing machine	vacuum cleaner		

J Review: Counting syllables ☐ ☐ ☐

1 Say each word. Write the number of syllables.

1. Canada   3
2. sofa
3. blanket
4. telephone
5. paper towels
6. television
7. freezer
8. alarm clock
9. carpet
10. refrigerator

2 Check your answers with the class.

K Linking with M

1 The sound **M** links to a vowel sound at the beginning of the next word. Listen.

Jim is.   Jimmmis .

Come on.   Comemmon .

2 The sound **M** links to another **M** sound at the beginning of the next word. Listen.

Tom may.   Tommmmay .

some more   somemmmore

3 Listen. Say each sentence two times.

1. Jim is here.   Jimmmis here.

2. What time is it?   What timemmis it?

3. Sam and I will go.   Sammmand I will go.

4. We want some more.   We want somemmmore .

5. Ice cream is cold.   Ice creammmis cold.

6. Tom may go home.   Tommmmay go home.

7. Turn the alarm off.   Turn the alarmmmoff .

8. She came much later.   She camemmmuch later.

L Past -ed ending

1 Usually, -ed is added for the past form of a verb. Listen.

Present + -ed = Past

rent   rented
need   needed
play   played
talk   talked

2 Say each word two times. Tap the syllables.

M *Extra syllable or not?* □ □ □

Sometimes -ed makes an extra syllable. But usually it does not.

1 Listen.

Present + -ed = Past

rent   rented
    □   □ □

need   needed
    □   □ □

talk   talked
    □   □

wash   washed
    □   □

listen   listened
    □ □   □   □

plan   planned
    □   □

2 Listen. Hold up one finger if you hear one syllable.
Hold up two fingers if you hear two syllables.

Final -t + -ed	Final -d + -ed	Other letters
painted	added	opened
rented	loaded	walked
counted	landed	cleaned
planted	needed	closed

3 Read these rules.

The Past Tense Syllable Rules

1. When a verb ends with -t or -d, -ed will be an extra syllable.

2. When a verb ends in any other letter, -ed will NOT be an extra syllable.

add   added   close   closed
  □   □ □   □   □

---

4 Write -ed after these verbs. Then say each word two times.

Extra syllable

1. want...............
2. end................
3. add................
4. repeat............
5. visit..............
6. wait...............
7. lift................

No extra syllable

8. rain...............
9. talk...............
10. wash..............
11. push..............
12. look..............
13. play..............
14. call..............

N *Pair work: Yesterday or every day?*

1 Student A, say sentence **a** or **b**.

2 Student B, say "Every day" for present or "Yesterday" for past.

3 Take turns saying sentences.

Examples

Student A: We plant flowers.
Student B: Every day.

Student B: We wanted a ride.
Student A: Yesterday.

1. a. We planted flowers.
   b. We plant flowers.

2. a. We wanted a ride.
   b. We want a ride.

3. a. I need more money.
   b. I needed more money.

4. a. We painted our kitchen.
   b. We paint our kitchen.

5. a. The planes landed at
       the airport.
   b. The planes land at
       the airport.

6. a. We wait for the train.
   b. We waited for the train.

7. a. We planned meals.
   b. We plan meals.

8. a. We washed our car.
   b. We wash our car.

9. a. They looked at pictures.
   b. They look at pictures.

10. a. The children play
        at school.
    b. The children played
        at school.

6 Weak syllables
Linking vowels

Can I help you?   Yes, I'd like a pizza.

A   Vowels in strong and weak syllables

Strong	Regular	Weak
a	a	ə
e	e	ə
i	i	ə
o	o	ə
u	u	ə
Very easy to hear	**Easy to hear**	Hard to hear

B   Rules for strong and weak syllables

1 Review these rules.

The Strong Syllable Rules

When you say a word alone:

1. Each word has one strong syllable.
2. The vowel in a strong syllable is long.

pa per   pen cil   comp u ter

When you say words in a sentence:

3. One word is the most important.
4. The vowel in the strong syllable of the important word is extra long.

I need a pencil .   I needed a pencil.

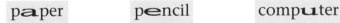

2 Read these new rules.

The Weak Syllable Rules

1. The vowels in some syllables keep their regular sound.
    But some syllables get weak.

2. The vowels in weak syllables are short and not clear.
3. All weak vowels sound the same.
4. The weak vowel sound is the most common sound in
    spoken English.

paper	pencil	computer
papər	pencəl	cəmputər

---

3 Listen.

1. salad   saləd
2. lemon   lemən
3. vanilla   vənillə
4. sandwich   sandwəch
5. lemonade   lemənade
6. tomato   təmato

C *Which vowel sounds are weak?*

1 Listen. Draw a line through the weak vowels.

1. bánaná
2. Canada
3. freezer
4. blanket
5. vanilla
6. China
7. Japan

2 Check your answers with the class.

Saying strong and weak syllables

Listen. Say each word two times.

Canada	America	Japan	China	Mexico
Canədə	əmerəcə	Jəpan	Chinə	Mexəco

🎧 **E**

Strong and weak syllables in food names

Listen. Say each word two times. Remember to make the strong vowels long and the weak vowels short.

1. tomato
   təmato

2. burger
   burgər

3. sesame bun
   sesəme bun

4. ketchup
   ketchəp

5. soda
   sodə

6. pizza
   pizzə

7. spaghetti
   spəghetti

8. pepperoni
   peppəroni

9. vanilla
   vənillə

10. chocolate
    choclət

🎧 **F**   Linking vowels

A vowel sound at the end of a word links to a vowel at the beginning of the next word.

Listen. Say each group of words two times.

1. coffee and milk   coffeeeand milk
2. tea and lemon   teaeeand lemon
3. pizza and salad   pizzaaaand salad
4. vanilla ice cream   vanillaaaice cream
5. banana or apple   bananaaaor apple

G   Weak "and"

Usually the word "and" is so weak that it sounds
like ǝn . Listen. Say each group of words two times.

1. coffee and cream

   cóffee ǝn crēam

2. tea and lemon

   tēa ǝn lemǝn

3. coffee and cake

   cóffee ǝn cāke

4. burger and fries

   burgǝr ǝn frīes

H   Weak "and," "of," and "a"

Listen to the weak sounds of "and," "of," and "a."
Say each group of words two times.

1. a cup of coffee

   ǝ cup ǝ cóffee

2. a bowl of soup

   ǝ bowl ǝ soup

3. a slice of pie

   ǝ slīce ǝ pīe

4. a slice of lemon pie

   ǝ slīce ǝ lemǝn pīe

5. a burger with cheese, ketchup, and fries

   ǝ burgǝr with chēese, ketchǝp, ǝn frīes

6. a pizza with cheese and tomatoes

   ǝ pīzzǝ with chēese ǝn tǝmātoes

7. a burger and tomato soup

   ǝ burgǝr ǝn tǝmātǝ soup

Review: The One Vowel Rule

1 Review this rule.

> ### The One Vowel Rule
>
> When there is only one vowel letter in a syllable:
>
> 1. The vowel letter does NOT say its alphabet name.
> 2. The vowel letter says its RELATIVE sound.
>
> This rule is true for many words.
>
> | can | pencil | finger | hot | summer |
> |------|--------|--------|------|--------|
> | Mack | Jenny | Kitty | John | Russ |

2 Listen. Say each word two times.

A	E	I	O	U
salad	lemon	milk	chocolate	bun
banana	egg	vanilla	bottle	butter
sandwich	ketchup	chicken	clock	mustard

🎧 **J** **Music of English** 🎵🎶

Listen. Say each sentence two times.

Cən I h**e**lp you?

Yes. I'd like ə p**i**zzə.

What s**i**ze?

Eləphənt-size!

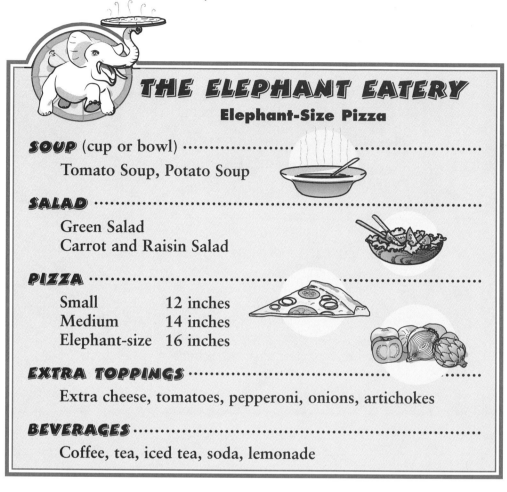

K The Elephant Eatery

Look at the menu. Listen. Say each food two times.

THE ELEPHANT EATERY
Elephant-Size Pizza

SOUP (cup or bowl) ....
Tomato Soup, Potato Soup

SALAD ....
Green Salad
Carrot and Raisin Salad

PIZZA ....
Small   12 inches
Medium   14 inches
Elephant-size 16 inches

EXTRA TOPPINGS ....
Extra cheese, tomatoes, pepperoni, onions, artichokes

BEVERAGES ....
Coffee, tea, iced tea, soda, lemonade

L Pair work: In the Elephant Eatery

1 Listen to the conversation.

2 Say the conversation with a partner. Take turns as the server and the customer.

Server: Can I help you?
Customer: Yes, I'd like a pizza and coffee.
Server: What kind of pizza? Plain, cheese, or with everything?
Customer: What's everything?
Server: Cheese, tomatoes, onions, pepperoni, and artichokes.
Customer: Great! I want one with everything!
Server: What size?
Customer: Elephant-size! I'm very hungry!

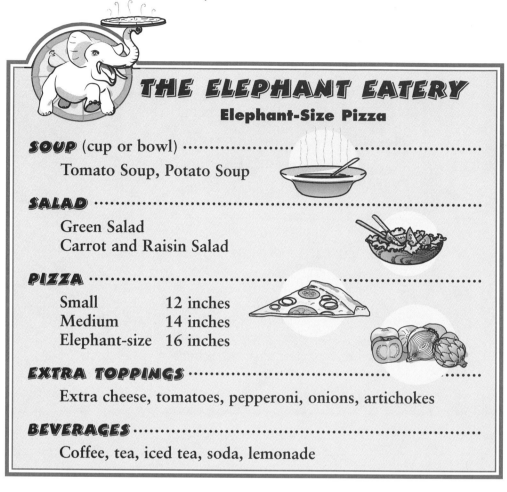

M Pair work: Ordering food

Order food from the Elephant Eatery menu. Take turns as the server and the customer.

Example

> Server: Can I help you?
> Customer: Yes, I'd like a pizza with pepperoni.
> Server: What size?
> Customer: Medium.
> Server: Okay. Anything else?
> Customer: A cup of coffee, please.
> Server: Coming right up!

N Food game   EXTRA

1 Divide into teams.

2 Write food words with your team.

3 Circle the strong syllable in each word.

4 After five minutes, compare your words. Each team gets one point for each correct answer.

Examples

(ca)rrot   (ce)lery   maca(ro)ni

7 The most important word

Are you going to eat supper at nine?
No, at six.

A The most important thing

Look at these pictures. What makes the rabbit easy to see?

Hard to see

Easy to see

> **Easy to see**
>
> The rabbit is easy to see when:
> - it jumps up
> - it is extra long
> - the rabbit is light, and the leaves are dark

B The most important word

1 What makes a word easy to hear?

> **Easy to hear**
>
> In English, a word is easy to hear when:
> - the strong syllable jumps up or down
> - the vowel in the strong syllable is extra long
> - the other words in the sentence are weak

2 Listen.

A: What's the matter?

B: I lost a ticket.

A: What's it for?

B: It's for a show.

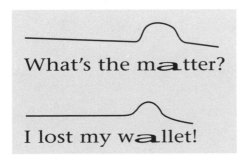

What's the m**a**tter?

I lost a t**i**cket.

What's it f**o**r?

It's for a sh**o**w.

3 Read these rules.

Rules for the Most Important Word

1. Each sentence has one most important word.

   What's the **matter**?

2. The vowel sound in the strong syllable of that word is extra long.

   What's the m**a**tter ?

3. The voice goes up or down on the strong syllable in the most important word.

   What's the m**a**tter?   What's the m**a**tter?

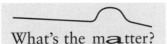 **C** *Music of English* 🎵🎵
_____

Listen. Say these sentences two times.

What's the m**a**tter?

I lost my w**a**llet!

D Pair work: The most important word

1 Listen to the conversations.

2 Say these conversations two times with a partner. Go up or down on the most important word.

1. The Glasses

Sue: What's the matter ? ("Matter" is the important word.)

Ted: I lost my glasses . ("Glasses" is the important word.)

Sue: What kind of glasses? ("Kind" is the important word.)

Ted: Reading glasses. ("Reading" is the important word.)

2. The Keys

Mike: What's the matter ? ("Matter" is the important word.)

Jane: I lost my keys . ("Keys" is the important word.)

Mike: Which keys? ("Which" is the important word.)

Jane: My car keys. ("Car" is the important word.)

E Pair work: Finding the most important word

1 Circle the most important word in each sentence.

2 Say these conversations two times with a partner.

1. The Shoes
   Jean: What's (wrong)?
   Joan: I lost my shoes.
   Jean: Which shoes?
   Joan: My tennis shoes.

2. The Dog

      Jim: What's the problem?

    Mike: I lost my dog.

      Jim: What kind of dog?

    Mike: A brown dog. A small brown dog.

      Jim: I saw a small brown dog. It was at the supermarket.

3. A Letter

      Bob: What are you doing?

  Jenny: I'm writing a letter.

      Bob: What kind of letter?

  Jenny: A business letter.

      Bob: What kind of business?

  Jenny: Personal business!

F *Music of English* ♫ ♪

Listen. Say each sentence two times.

California is a cíty.

No it ísn't. It's a státe.

Lemons are swéet.

No they áren't. Hóney is sweet.

G *Pair work: Disagreement*

1 Circle the most important word in each sentence.

2 Say these conversations two times with a partner. Go up or down on the strong syllable in the important word.

1. A: California is a (city).
   B: No it isn't. It's a (state).

2. A: Ice is hot.
   B: No it isn't. It's cold.

3. A: Lemons are sweet.
   B: No they aren't. Honey is sweet.

4. A: Babies are bigger than children.
   B: No they aren't. They're smaller than children.

5. A: Fish eat grass.
   B: No they don't. They eat smaller fish.

6. A: The world is flat.
   B: No it isn't. It's round.

7. A: You buy books at a library.
   B: No you don't. You buy books at a bookstore.

8. A: You borrow books at a bookstore.
   B: No you don't. You borrow books at a library.

9. A: Cars travel in the air.
   B: No they don't. They travel on the road.

10. A: Toronto is the capital of Canada.
    B: No it isn't. Ottawa is the capital of Canada.

H *Music of English* ♫♪

Listen. Say each sentence two times.

I wanted a cup of t**e**a.

Not c**o**ffee?

I wanted a c**u**p of soup.

Not a b**o**wl?

I *Pair work: Misunderstandings*

1 Customer, say **a** or **b**.

2 Server, answer.

3 Take turns as the customer and server.

Examples

Customer: I wanted **two** lemonades.
Server: Not one?
Customer: I wanted a cup of **soup**.
Server: Not coffee?

Customer	Server
1. a. I wanted a cup of **soup**.	Not coffee?
b. I wanted a **cup** of soup.	Not a bowl?
2. a. I wanted **two** lemonades.	Not one?
b. I wanted two **lemonades**.	Not Cokes?

3. a. But I wanted lemon **pie**!   Not ice cream?
   b. But I wanted **lemon** pie!   Not apple?

4. a. I asked for potato **salad**.   Not soup?
   b. I asked for **potato** salad.   Not tomato?

5. a. This is a tuna **sandwich**!   Oh, did you want
                                        tuna salad?
   b. This is a **tuna** sandwich!   Oh, did you
                                        want egg?

6. a. That's a **small** glass!   Oh, I thought you
                                    wanted a small glass.
   b. That's a small **glass**!   Oh, did you want
                                    a cup?

J   Music of English

Listen. Say each sentence two times.

Are you going to eat supper at n**i**ne?

No, at s**i**x.

Are you going to get up at s**e**ven?

No, at t**e**n.

K *Pair work: Correcting a mistake about time*

1 Student A, ask a question about an activity from the Activities box below. Use any time of day.

2 Student B, say "No" and give another time.

3 Take turns asking questions. Remember to go up or down on the important word.

Examples

> Student A: Are you going to get up at seven?
> Student B: No, at **nine**.
>
> Student B: Are you going to meet a friend at one?
> Student A: No, at **two**.

Activities

eat breakfast	get up	catch a bus
eat lunch	go to work	meet a friend
eat supper	have a snack	go to bed

L *Review: Counting syllables* ☐ ☐ ☐

1 Listen. Write the number of syllables.

1. Monday ....2.......
2. Tuesday ....
3. Wednesday ....
4. Thursday ....
5. Friday ....
6. Saturday ....
7. Sunday ....

2 Check your answers with the class.

M Pair work: Correcting a mistake about the day

1 Student A, ask a question about an activity from the Activities box. Choose any day.

2 Student B, say "No" and give another day.

3 Take turns asking questions.

Examples

Student A: Are you going to see the doctor on Monday?
Student B: No, **Friday**.

Student B: Are you going to play soccer on Thursday?
Student A: No, **Saturday**.

Activities

see the doctor	study English	play soccer
visit friends	go to class	wash your car
bake a cake	shop for clothes	buy a car
fly to New York	write a letter	wash the dog

Days

Monday	Friday
Tuesday	Saturday
Wednesday	Sunday
Thursday	

8

Stop sound T/D and continuing sound S/Z
Linking with T/D and S/Z

How do you spell "cakes"?
Is she running? No, she's reading.

A Stop sounds and continuing sounds

1 Look at these pictures.

Stop sound T/D   Continuing sound S/Z

Looking to the front

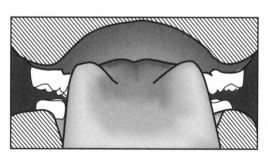

Looking down

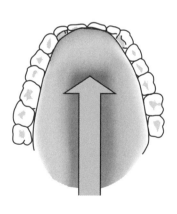
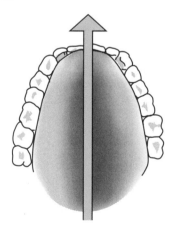

but   busss

Air stops   Air continues

2 Listen for the sound at the end of each word. Do not say the words.

1. but   bus
   but   busss

2. boat   boats
   boat   boatsss

3. had   has
   had   hazzz

4. seat   seats
   seat   seatsss

5. it   is
   it   izzz

6. hit   his
   hit   hizzz

7. coat   coats
   coat   coatsss

B *Which word is different?*

1 Listen. Mark the different word.

	X	Y	Z	
1.	....	....	✔	(right, right, rice)
2.	....	....	....	
3.	....	....	....	
4.	....	....	....	
5.	....	....	....	
6.	....	....	....	
7.	....	....	....	
8.	....	....	....	

2 Listen again.

C Which word do you hear?

1 Listen. Circle the word you hear.

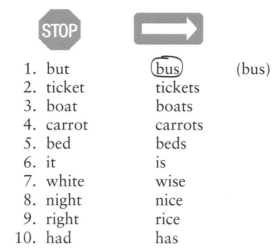

	STOP	→	
1.	but	(bus)	(bus)
2.	ticket	tickets	
3.	boat	boats	
4.	carrot	carrots	
5.	bed	beds	
6.	it	is	
7.	white	wise	
8.	night	nice	
9.	right	rice	
10.	had	has	

2 Listen again.

D Final sounds: Stop or continue?

1 Cover the words.

2 Listen to each word. Mark if the final sound stops or continues.

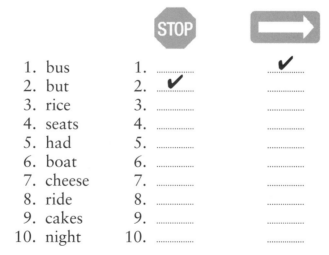

		STOP		→
1.	bus	1.		✔
2.	but	2. ✔		
3.	rice	3.		
4.	seats	4.		
5.	had	5.		
6.	boat	6.		
7.	cheese	7.		
8.	ride	8.		
9.	cakes	9.		
10.	night	10.		

3 Look at the words. Listen again.

E   Pair work: Is it one or more than one?

1 Student A, say word **a** or **b**.

2 Student B, if you hear a word meaning one thing, hold up one finger. If you hear a word meaning more than one thing, hold up all five fingers.

3 Take turns saying words.

Examples

Student A: Carrots.
Student B: (Hold up all five fingers.)

Student B: Jacket.
Student A: (Hold up one finger.)

1. a. carrot
    b. carrots

2. a. jackets
    b. jacket

3. a. fruit
    b. fruits

4. a. postcard
    b. postcards

5. a. coats
    b. coat

6. a. lemonade
    b. lemonades

7. a. ticket
    b. tickets

8. a. shake
    b. shakes

9. a. Coke
    b. Cokes

10. a. seat
    b. seats

F   Music of English ♫♪

Listen. Say each sentence two times.

How do you spell "fr**u**it"?

How do you spell "c**a**kes"?

G *Pair work: How do you spell "hats"?*

1 Student A, ask question **a** or **b**.

2 Student B, spell the word.

3 Student A, if the spelling is correct, say "Right." If it is wrong, say the word again.

4 Take turns asking questions.

Examples

Student A: How do you spell "hats"?
Student B: H - A - T - S.
Student A: Right.

Student B: How do you spell "beds"?
Student A: B - E - D.
Student B: No, "beds."
Student A: B - E - D - S.

1. a. How do you spell "hat"? H - A - T.
   b. How do you spell "hats"? H - A - T - S.

2. a. How do you spell "beds"? B - E - D - S.
   b. How do you spell "bed"? B - E - D.

3. a. How do you spell "fruit"? F - R - U - I - T.
   b. How do you spell "fruits"? F - R - U - I - T - S.

4. a. How do you spell "white"? W - H - I - T - E.
   b. How do you spell "wise"? W - I - S - E.

5. a. How do you spell "suit"? S - U - I - T.
   b. How do you spell "suits"? S - U - I - T - S.

6. a. How do you spell "plate"? P - L - A - T - E.
   b. How do you spell "plays"? P - L - A - Y - S.

7. a. How do you spell "right"? R - I - G - H - T.
   b. How do you spell "rice"? R - I - C - E.

8. a. How do you spell "repeat"? R - E - P - E - A -T.
   b. How do you spell "repeats"? R - E - P - E - A - T - S.

H Linking with T/D ⊂━○━⊃━○━⊃━○━⊃

T/D is a stop sound. It links to a vowel at the beginning of the next word.

1 Listen.

bad apples   badapples

Great idea!   Greatidea !

Find it.   Findit .

2 Listen. Say each sentence two times.

1. These are bad apples.   These are badapples .
2. That's a great idea.   That's a greatidea .
3. Please find it.   Please findit .
4. This food is hot.   This foodis hot.
5. They counted all the money.   They countedall the money.
6. That blanket is clean.   That blanketis clean.
7. We tried every key.   We triedevery key.
8. That cat eats cheese.   That cateats cheese.

I Linking with S/Z ⊂━○━⊃━○━⊃━○━⊃

S/Z is a continuing sound. A continuing sound links to a vowel sound at the beginning of the next word. It also links to other continuing sounds.

1 Listen.

Ann's address   Annzzzaddress

Gus said.   Gusssaid .

This is Ann.   ThisssizzzAnn .

2 Listen. Say each group of words two times.

1. They ordered cakes and coffee.   They ordered cakesssand coffee.
2. Gus said, "Hello!"   Gusssaid , "Hello!"
3. The books are on the shelf.   The booksssare on the shelf.

4. Put the plates on the table.   Put the platessson the table.

5. I have tickets in my pocket.   I have ticketsssin my pocket.

6. It's so big!   Itsssso big!

7. It's stuff for the house.   Itsssstuff for the house.

8. Ann's address is new.   Annzzzaddresssssizzznew .

9. She's never here.   Shezzznever here.

10. His mother's always late.   Hizzzmotherzzzalways late.

J Review: The Two Vowel Rule

> **The Two Vowel Rule**
>
> When there are two vowel letters in a syllable:
>
>   1. The first vowel says its alphabet name.
>   2. The second vowel is silent.
>
> cake   tea   ice   cone   cube

1 These words have two vowel letters together. Listen and
say each word two times.

A^y	E^y	I^y	O^w	U^w
paid	reach	fries	boat	blue
train	need	cries	soak	fruit
plain	easy	tried	throat	true
explain	freezer	pies	coach	cue
remain	reason	applied	toe	barbecue
complain	reading	replied	loan	suitcase

2 These words have a silent letter -e at the end. Listen and
say each word two times.

A^y	E^y	I^y	O^w	U^w
plane	these	price	note	cute
change	complete	retire	clothes	reduce
arrange	extreme	arrive	those	excuse
erase	Chinese	advice	telephone	refuse

K Music of English ♫♪

Listen. Say each sentence two times.

Is she ru**n**ning?

No, she's r**ea**ding.

Is he playing t**e**nnis?

Yes, he **i**s.

L Pair work: Correcting a mistake

1 Listen. Say the names of these activities.

running	drinking water
sleeping	playing tennis
reading	playing soccer
eating	playing basketball

2 Student A, point to a picture in the Activities box on the next page. Ask a question about the picture.

3 Student B, answer.

4 Take turns asking questions.

Examples

Student A: Is she drinking water?
Student B: Yes, she is. (or) No, she's **eating**.

Student B: Is she playing basketball?
Student A: Yes, she is. (or) No, she's playing **tennis**.

Activities

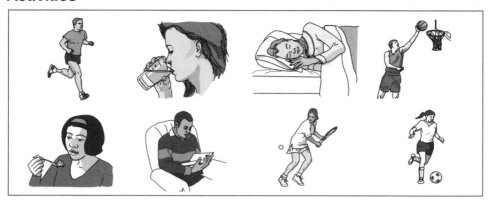

M *S-Ball game*

1 Divide into groups of four or five. Each group has a small ball. One student is the leader.

2 Leader, ask a question and then throw the ball to a student.

3 Student, catch the ball and answer the question. If you answer correctly (with a final **S** sound in the verb), you become the new leader.

Examples

Leader:	What does "writer" mean?
	(Throw the ball to a student.)
Student A:	A person who writes.
	(Student A becomes the leader.)
Leader:	What does "baker" mean?
	(Throw the ball to a student.)
Student B:	A person who bake.
Leader:	No. What does "baker" mean?
	(Throw the ball to a different student.)
Student C:	A person who bakes.

1. What does "writer" mean?
2. What does "baker" mean?
3. What does "worker" mean?
4. What does "reader" mean?
5. What does "cleaner" mean?
6. What does "leader" mean?
7. What does "speaker" mean?
8. What does "player" mean?
9. What does "painter" mean?
10. What does "trainer" mean?

9 Final sounds D and L
Linking with L

How do you spell "whale"?
What does "paid" mean?

 A **_Final sounds D and L_**

1 Look at these pictures.

Stop sound D   Continuing sound L

Looking to the front

 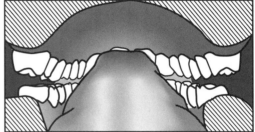

Looking down

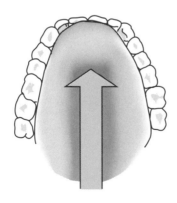 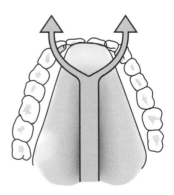

bed   bellll

Air stops   Air continues

2 Listen for the sound at the end of each word.
Do not say the words.

	STOP	→
1.	food	fool
	food	foolll
2.	made	mail
	made	mailll
3.	road	roll
	road	rollll
4.	feed	feel
	feed	feelll
5.	bed	bell
	bed	bellll

B *Which word is different?*

1 Listen. Mark the different word.

	X	Y	Z	
1.	....	....	✔	(food, food, fool)
2.	....	....	....	
3.	....	....	....	
4.	....	....	....	
5.	....	....	....	
6.	....	....	....	
7.	....	....	....	
8.	....	....	....	

2 Listen again.

C Which word do you hear?

1 Listen. Circle the word you hear.

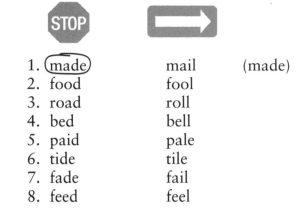

	STOP	→	
1.	(made)	mail	(made)
2.	food	fool	
3.	road	roll	
4.	bed	bell	
5.	paid	pale	
6.	tide	tile	
7.	fade	fail	
8.	feed	feel	

2 Listen again.

D Saying final sounds D and L

Listen. Say each word two times.

	STOP	→
1.	food	foolll
2.	made	mailll
3.	road	rollll
4.	feed	feelll
5.	bed	bellll

E Music of English 🎵

Listen. Say each sentence two times.

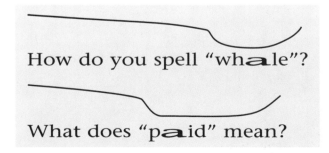

How do you spell "wh**a**le"?

What does "p**a**id" mean?

F   *Pair work: Hearing and saying final D and L*

1 Student A, ask question **a** or **b**.

2 Student B, answer.

3 Student A, if the answer is correct, say "Right." If it is wrong, ask again.

4 Take turns asking questions.

Examples

> Student A: How do you spell "made"?
> Student B: M - A - I - L.
> Student A: No, "made."
> Student B: M - A - D - E.
>
> Student B: What does "fool" mean?
> Student A: A silly person.
> Student B: Right.

1. a. How do you spell "made"?   M - A - D - E.
   b. How do you spell "mail"?   M - A - I - L.

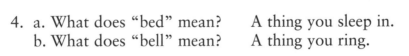

2. a. What does "food" mean?   Something to eat.
   b. What does "fool" mean?   A silly person.

3. a. How do you spell "road"?   R - O - A - D.
   b. How do you spell "roll"?   R - O - L - L.

4. a. What does "bed" mean?   A thing you sleep in.
   b. What does "bell" mean?   A thing you ring.

5. a. How do you spell "bed"?   B - E - D.
   b. How do you spell "bell"?   B - E - L - L.

6. a. What does "whale" mean?   A very big sea animal.
   b. What does "wade" mean?   To walk in water.

7. a. How do you spell "whale"?   W - H - A - L - E.
   b. How do you spell "wade"?   W - A - D - E.

8. a. What does "feed" mean?   To give food.
   b. What does "feel" mean?   To touch something.

9. a. How do you spell "feed"?   F - E - E - D.
   b. How do you spell "feel"?   F - E - E - L.

10. a. What does "paid" mean?   The past of "pay."
    b. What does "pail" mean?   A bucket.

G Listening for final L: Present or future?

1 Cover the sentences. Listen. Mark if the sentence is present or future.

2 Look at the sentences. Listen again.

	Present	Future
1. a. I read the newspaper. b. I'll read the newspaper.		✔
2. a. I drink coffee. b. I'll drink coffee.		
3. a. I drive to work. b. I'll drive to work.		
4. a. I take the train. b. I'll take the train.		
5. a. We ride the bus. b. We'll ride the bus.		
6. a. They go home. b. They'll go home.		
7. a. We watch TV. b. We'll watch TV.		
8. a. They go to the movies. b. They'll go to the movies.		

H Pair work: Present or future?

1 Listen. Say these words two times.

Present	Future
every day	tomorrow
every night	tonight
every week	next week

2 Student A, say sentence **a** or **b**.

3 Student B, say an answer from the box above.

4 Take turns saying sentences.

Examples

Student A: We eat cake.
Student B: Every night.

Student B: We'll ask questions.
Student A: Tonight.

1. a. We eat cake.
   b. We'll eat cake.

2. a. We ask questions.
   b. We'll ask questions.

3. a. They cut the bread.
   b. They'll cut the bread.

4. a. They go to the store.
   b. They'll go to the store.

5. a. I buy fish.
   b. I'll buy fish.

6. a. I cook dinner.
   b. I'll cook dinner.

7. a. We read the newspaper.
   b. We'll read the newspaper.

8. a. We work hard.
   b. We'll work hard.

I Linking with L

L is a continuing sound. A continuing sound links to another continuing sound or a vowel sound at the beginning of the next word.

1 Listen.

Sell it. Sellllit .

Tell me. Tellllme .

2 Listen. Say each sentence two times.

1. Sell it now. Sellllit now.
2. Tell us everything. Tellllus everything.
3. Do you feel okay? Do you feelllokay ?
4. Will you go? Willllyou go?
5. How do you spell "whale?" How do you spellllwhale ?
6. These books are all new. These books are allllnew .
7. Tell me all you know. Tellllme allllyou know.
8. Tom will look for the key. Tom willlllook for the key.

J Review: Counting syllables in sentences ▢ ▢ ▢

1 Cover the sentences.

2 Listen. Say each sentence.

3 Write the number of syllables.

1. Make a bowl of rice.   1. _5_
2. We need two plates.   2. _____
3. They like ice cubes.   3. _____
4. Joe needed five tickets.   4. _____
5. We cleaned the plates.   5. _____

4 Read the sentences aloud. Check your answers.

10 Final sounds L and LD
Linking with all the stop sounds

Did you say "coal"? No, I said "cold."

 A ___Final Sounds L and LD___

Listen to the final sounds in these words.

1. call	called
2. pull	pulled
3. mail	mailed
4. bowl	bold
5. sail	sailed
6. fill	filled
7. coal	cold

B ___Present and past___

1 Read the sentences.

2 Cover the sentences.

3 Listen. Mark Past or Present.

		Present	Past	
1.	I called a friend.	1.	✔	(called)
2.	I sail a boat on Sundays.	2.	....	
3.	We mail a letter every day.	3.	....	
4.	We mailed everything.	4.	....	
5.	We fill our glasses.	5.	....	
6.	A cow made our milk.	6.	....	
7.	We sealed all the letters.	7.	....	

4 Look at the sentences. Listen again.

C   *Pair work: What does "mail" mean?*

1 Student A, ask question **a** or **b**.

2 Student B, answer.

3 Take turns asking questions.

Examples

Student A: What does "mail" mean?
Student B: Things like letters and postcards.

Student B: What does "pulled" mean?
Student A: The past of "pull."

1. a. What does "made" mean?   The past of "make."
    b. What does "mail" mean?   Things like letters
                                     and postcards.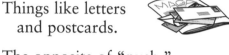

2. a. What does "pull" mean?   The opposite of "push."
    b. What does "pulled" mean?   The past of "pull."

3. a. What does "feel" mean?   To touch.
    b. What does "field" mean?   Open land.

4. a. How do you spell "while"?   W - H - I - L - E.
    b. How do you spell "wild"?   W - I - L - D.

5. a. What does "sold" mean?   The past of "sell."
    b. What does "sole" mean?   The bottom of a shoe.

6. a. What does "goal" mean?   Winning a point
                                     in soccer.
    b. What does "gold" mean?   A yellow metal.

7. a. What does "coal" mean?   A black rock that burns.
    b. What does "cold" mean?   The opposite of "hot."

8. a. What does "mild" mean?   Not strong.
    b. What does "mile" mean?   Five thousand two
                                     hundred and eighty feet.

9. a. How do you spell "smile"?   S - M - I - L - E.
    b. How do you spell "smiled"?   S - M - I - L - E - D.

10. a. What does "smiled" mean?   The past of "smile."
    b. What does "smile" mean?   To turn up your lips.

Pair work: Present and past

1 Listen. Say these words two times.

Present	Past
every day	yesterday
every week	last week
usually	last year
often	two days ago
always	last night

2 Student A, say sentence **a** or **b**.

3 Student B, say an answer from the box above.

4 Take turns saying sentences.

Examples

Student A: I call home.
Student B: Every day.

Student B: We filled the gas tank.
Student A: Yesterday.

1. a. I called home.
    b. I call home.

2. a. We filled the gas tank.
    b. We fill the gas tank.

3. a. We sail on the lake.
    b. We sailed on the lake.

4. a. Babies spill milk.
    b. Babies spilled milk.

5. a. The boys fail every test.
    b. The boys failed every test.

6. a. They smile a lot.
    b. They smiled a lot.

7. a. I mailed a letter.
    b. I mail a letter.

8. a. They spelled all the words.
    b. They spell all the words.

E Music of English 🎵🎵

Listen. Say each sentence two times.

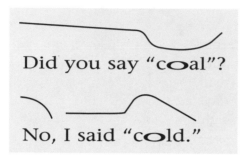

Did you say "coal"?

No, I said "cold."

F Pair work: Did you say "made"?

1 Student A, say a word from the Words box below.

2 Student B, pretend you heard a different word and ask,
"Did you say ....?"

3 Student A, correct Student B and answer,
"No, I said ...."

4 Take turns saying words.

Examples

> Student A: Mail.
> Student B: Did you say "made"?
> Student A: No, I said "mail."
>
> Student B: Field.
> Student A: Did you say "feel"?
> Student B: No, I said "field."

Words

mail	made	feel	field
spell	spelled	bowl	bold
pull	pulled	while	wild
sail	sailed	goal	gold

G Linking stop sounds to vowels

In English, the stop sounds are **T/D**, **B/P**, and **K/G**.
A stop sound links to a vowel at the beginning
of the next word.

1 Listen to the stop sounds **T** and **D**. Say each sentence
two times.

1. We paid it.	We paidit .
2. Sit on it.	Siton it.
3. Hold it.	Holdit .
4. Find it.	Findit .
5. Is it cold or hot?	Is it coldor hot?
6. We had a lot of money.	We hada lotof money.

2 Listen to the stop sounds **B**, **P**, **K**, and **G**. Say each sentence
two times.

1. The taxicab is coming.	The taxicabis coming.
2. I want a tub of butter.	I want a tubof butter.
3. Ask everybody.	Askeverybody .
4. Cook all the food.	Cookall the food.
5. Thank you.	Thankyou .
6. Help us.	Helpus .
7. Link all vowels.	Linkall vowels.
8. A cup of coffee, please.	A cupof coffee, please.
9. Stop it.	Stopit .
10. Tap each syllable.	Tapeach syllable.
11. We keep all mail.	We keepall mail.
12. This is a bag of oranges.	This is a bagof oranges.

11

Final sounds T/D and R
Linking with R

What is it? Where is it?

A   *Final sounds T/D and R*

1 Look at these pictures.

Stop sound T/D   Continuing sound R

Looking to the front

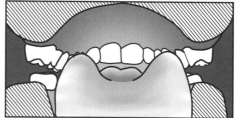

Looking down

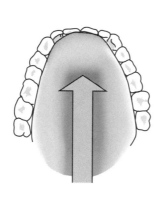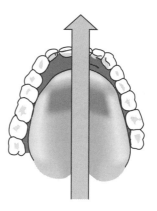

Looking to the side

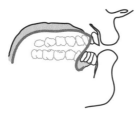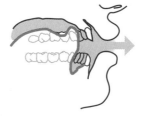

bet   bed   bearrr

2 Listen for the final sound. Do not say the words.

	STOP	→
1.	bad	bar
	bad	barrr
2.	fat	far
	fat	farrr
3.	feed	fear
	feed	fearrr
4.	fade	fair
	fade	fairrr
5.	card	car
	card	carrr
6.	art	are
	art	arerr
7.	what	where
	what	whererr

B *Which word is different?*

1 Listen. Mark the different word.

	X	Y	Z	
1.	....	....	✔	(bed, bed, bear)
2.	....	....	....	
3.	....	....	....	
4.	....	....	....	
5.	....	....	....	
6.	....	....	....	

2 Listen again.

C *Which word do you hear?*

1 Listen. Circle the word you hear.

1. (bed)   bear   (bed)
2. art   are
3. card   car
4. shared   share
5. fired   fire
6. what   where
7. cat   car
8. feared   fear
9. bad   bar
10. feet   fear

2 Listen again.

D *Saying final sounds T/D and R*

Listen. Say each word two times.

1. fat   far
2. cat   car
3. tide   tire
4. fade   fair
5. paid   pair
6. what   where
7. card   car
8. art   are
9. feared   fear
10. cared   care

Pair work: Present and past

Present		Past	
every day	often	yesterday	two days ago
every week	always	last week	last night
usually		last year	

1 Student A, say sentence **a** or **b**.

2 Student B, say an answer from the box above.

3 Take turns saying sentences.

Examples

Student A: They shared everything.	Student B: I care about my work.
Student B: Yesterday.	Student A: Always.

1. a. They share everything.
   b. They shared everything.

2. a. I care about my work.
   b. I cared about my work.

3. a. They prepare their lessons.
   b. They prepared their lessons.

4. a. They feared everything.
   b. They fear everything.

5. a. We repaired cars.
   b. We repair cars.

6. a. Snakes scared me.
   b. Snakes scare me.

7. a. I adore her.
   b. I adored her.

8. a. Lions roar.
   b. Lions roared.

F Linking with R

R is a continuing sound. It links to a vowel or another continuing sound at the beginning of the next word.

1 Listen. Say these words two times.

far away	farrraway
hear me	hearrrme
Peter knows	Peterrrknows

2 Listen. Say each sentence two times.

1. He is far away.   He's farrraway .
2. Where is it?   Whererris it?
3. What are all those things?   What arerrall those things?
4. Peter knows the answer.   Peterrrknows the answer.
5. Did you hear me?   Did you hearrrme ?
6. Are many people going?   Arerrmany people going?
7. Her voice is beautiful.   Herrrvoice is beautiful.
8. You're an hour late.   Yourerran hourrrlate .

G Linking with R, T/D, and L

Listen. Say each sentence two times.

1. I had a sandwich.   I hada sandwich.
2. Will everybody come?   Willlleverybody come?
3. Where are you?   Whererrarerryou ?
4. What is it?   Whatis it?
5. I heard everything.   I heardeverything .
6. Is it hard or soft?   Is it hardor soft?
7. The letter never arrived.   The letterrrneverrrarrived .
8. Jill is reading.   Jillllis reading.
9. We care about our work.   We carerrabouttourrrwork .
10. Put your hat on.   Put your haton .

H   *Pair work: What does "roar" mean?*

1 Student A, ask question **a** or **b**.

2 Student B, answer.

3 Student A, if the answer is correct, say "Right." If it is wrong, ask again.

4 Take turns asking questions.

Examples

> Student A: What does "roared" mean?
> Student B: The past of "roar."
> Student A: Right.
>
> Student B: What does "adore" mean?
> Student A: The past of "love."
> Student B: No. What does "adore" mean?
> Student A: Love.

1. a. What does "roar" mean?   The noise of a lion.
   b. What does "roared" mean?   The past of "roar."

2. a. What does "adore" mean?   Love.
   b. What does "adored" mean?   The past of "love."

3. a. What does "repair" mean?   To fix.
   b. What does "repaired" mean?   The past of "repair."

4. a. How do you spell "feared"?   F - E - A - R - E - D.
   b. How do you spell "fear"?   F - E - A - R.

5. a. How do you spell "art"?   A - R - T.
   b. How do you spell "are"?   A - R - E.

6. a. What does "pair" mean?   Two.
   b. What does "paid" mean?   The past of "pay."

7. a. How do you spell "her"?   H - E - R.
   b. How do you spell "hurt"?   H - U - R - T.

8. a. What does "near" mean?   Not far.
   b. What does "neat" mean?   Not messy.

9. a. How do you spell "fire"?   F - I - R - E.
   b. How do you spell "fight"?   F - I - G - H - T.

10. a. How do you spell "tire"?   T - I - R - E.
    b. How do you spell "tight"?   T - I - G - H - T.

I Music of English 🎵🎵

Listen. Say each sentence two times. Be careful with
the final sound of "where" and "what."

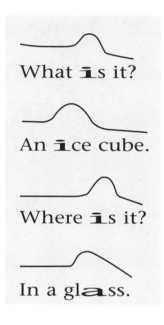

What **i**s it?

An **i**ce cube.

Where **i**s it?

In a gl**a**ss.

J Pair work: What is it? Where is it?

1 Student A, point to a picture on the next page and ask,
"What is it?" or "Where is it?"

2 Student B, say an answer from the box on the next page.

3 Take turns asking questions.

Examples

Student A: (Point to elephant.) What is it?
Student B: An elephant.

Student B: Where is it?
Student A: In a zoo.

What?	Where?
A cat.	On a chair.
An elephant.	Under a sofa.
An ice cube.	On a desk.
A flag.	On a flagpole.
A jacket.	In a zoo.
A pot.	In a glass.
A computer.	On a stove.

K *Music of English* ♫♪

Listen. Say each sentence two times.

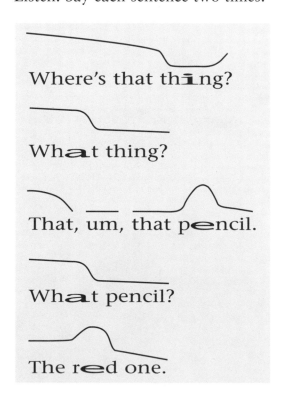

Where's that thing?

What thing?

That, um, that pencil.

What pencil?

The red one.

1 Listen.

2 Say the conversation with a partner. Take turns as Sue and Joe.

Sue: Where's my stuff?
Joe: **What** stuff?
Sue: That, um, that cheese.
Joe: **Which** cheese?
Sue: The cheese I put in the fridge.
Joe: **When**?
Sue: Last month.
Joe: Oh, **that** cheese! I threw it away!

12 Continuing sounds and stop sounds + S/Z
Linking with S/Z

What's a bank for?
Where's the library? It's on Main Street.

 A ___Review: Final sounds T/D and S/Z___

Listen. Say these words two times.

1. but   bus
   but   busss

2. it   is
   it   izzz

3. had   has
   had   hazzz

 B ___Do you hear a final S/Z sound?___

1 Listen. Mark Yes or No.

	Yes	No	
1.	✔	.....	(bus)
2.	.....	.....	
3.	.....	.....	
4.	.....	.....	
5.	.....	.....	
6.	.....	.....	
7.	.....	.....	
8.	.....	.....	
9.	.....	.....	
10.	.....	.....	

2 Listen again.

The English stop sounds are **T/D, P/B,** and **K/G.**

1 Listen. Circle the word you hear.

STOP	STOP + S/Z

1. cab   (cabs)

     cab   cabzzz

2. bank   banks

     bank   banksss

3. bag   bags

     bag   bagzzz

4. stop   stops

     stop   stopsss

5. supermarket   supermarkets

     supermarket   supermarketsss

6. laundromat   laundromats

     laundromat   laundromatsss

7. road   roads

     road   roadzzz

8. street   streets

     street   streetsss

9. shop   shops

     shop   shopsss

10. parking lot   parking lots

     parking lot   parking lotsss

2 Listen again.

D *Continuing sounds + S/Z*

1 Listen. Circle the word you hear.

➡️　　　　　　➡️ + S/Z

1. (plan)　　　　　plans
   plannn　　　　　planzzz

2. school　　　　　schools
   schoolll　　　　schoolzzz

3. hospital　　　　hospitals
   hospitalll　　　hospitalzzz

4. store　　　　　stores
   storerr　　　　storezzz

5. video　　　　　videos
   videooo　　　　videozzz

6. toy　　　　　　toys
   toyyy　　　　　toyzzz

7. city　　　　　cities
   cityyy　　　　citiezzz

8. avenue　　　　avenues
   avenueuu　　　avenuezzz

9. drive　　　　　drives
   drivevv　　　　drivezzz

10. alley　　　　alleys
    alleyyy　　　alleyzzz

2 Listen again.

E *Pair work: Is it one or more than one?*

1 Student A, say a word from the Places box.

2 Student B, if you hear a word meaning one place, hold up one finger. If you hear a word meaning more than one place, hold up all five fingers.

3 Student A, if the answer is correct, say "Right." If it is wrong, say the word again.

4 Take turns saying words.

Examples

Student A: Banks.
Student B: (Hold up all five fingers.)
Student A: Right.

Student B: Hospitals.
Student A: (Hold up one finger.)
Student B: No, "hospitals."

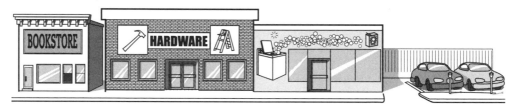

Places

park	parking lot	theaters	parking lots
laundromat	hospitals	school	bookstores
apartments	schools	bank	parks
toy department	drugstore	hospital	bookstore
video shop	banks	shops	

Remember that **S/Z** links to vowels and to other continuing sounds.

Listen. Say each sentence two times.

1. The shops‿are downtown. The shopsssare downtown.

2. The roads‿are full of traffic. The roadzzzare full of traffic.

3. The parking lots‿are full of cars. The parking lotsssare full of cars.

4. The banks‿are closed today. The banksssare closed today.

5. Are the shops‿open? Are the shopsssopen ?

6. Supermarkets‿are always‿open. Supermarketsssare alwayzzzopen .

7. The schools‿may be open. The schoolzzzmay be open.

8. Taxicabs‿never wait here. Taxicabzzznever wait here.

9. Toy shops‿sell toys. Toy shopsssssell toys.

10. Restaurants‿serve food. Restaurantsssserve food.

🎧 **G** **Music of English** 🎵🎶

Listen. Say each sentence two times. Go up or down on the most important word.

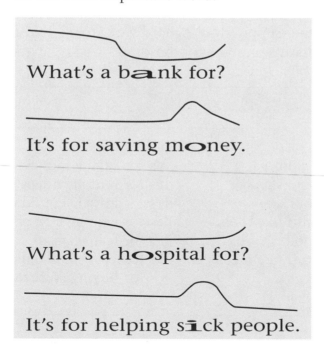

What's a b**a**nk for?

It's for saving m**o**ney.

What's a h**o**spital for?

It's for helping s**i**ck people.

H *Pair work: What's a bank for?*

1 Student A, look at the Places box. Ask what one of the places is for.

2 Student B, say an answer from the Answers box.

3 Take turns asking questions.

Examples

> Student A: What's a library for?
> Student B: It's for borrowing books.
>
> Student B: What's a toy store for?
> Student A: It's for buying toys.

Places

park	supermarket	bookstore	high school
bank	toy store	restaurant	preschool
video shop	auto supply store	hardware store	post office
drugstore	library	hospital	parking lot
laundromat			

Answers

It's for eating.	It's for mail.
It's for washing clothes.	It's for saving money.
It's for buying books.	It's for renting videos.
It's for buying toys.	It's for borrowing books.
It's for buying stuff like tools.	It's for helping sick people.
It's for buying food.	It's for teenagers.
It's for buying stuff like medicine.	It's for very small children.
It's for trees and grass.	It's for buying stuff for the car.
	It's for cars.

I   Music of English ♪♫

Listen. Say each sentence two times.

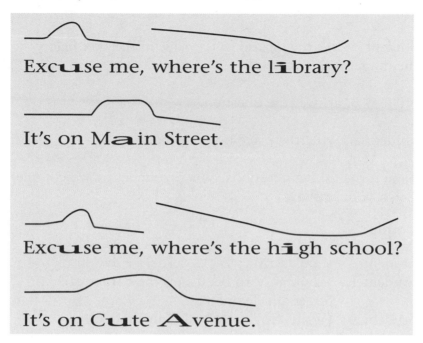

Exc**u**se me, where's the l**i**brary?

It's on M**a**in Street.

Exc**u**se me, where's the h**i**gh school?

It's on C**u**te **A**venue.

J   Pair work: Giving locations

1 Listen. Find the places on the map.

Visitor: Excuse me, where's the bookstore?
Resident: It's on the corner of Main and Jen.
Visitor: Is it near the library?
Resident: Yes, it's just across the street.
Visitor: And where is Jen Street?
Resident: It's one block south of Jean Street.
Visitor: Thanks a lot for your help.
Resident: No problem.

2 Say the conversation with
a partner. Take turns as
the visitor and the resident.

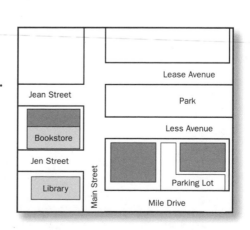

K *Pair work: Map game*

1 Ask about locations. Student A looks at Map A on page 89. Student B looks at Map B on page 90.

2 Student A, ask the location of a place in the box below the map.

3 Student B, answer the question.

4 Student A, write the place on your map.

5 Take turns asking questions. When your maps are complete, check your answers.

Example

> Student A: (Look at Map A.) Where's the toy store?
> Student B: (Look at Map B.) It's on the corner of Main Street and Jean Street.
> Student A: (Write "toy store" on your map.)

Map A

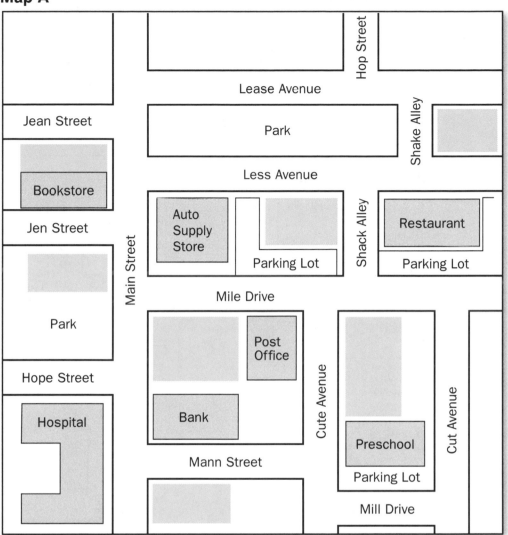

Student A, ask the location of the places in the box.

Places for Map A

toy store	high school
video shop	drugstore
hardware store	library
supermarket	

Map B

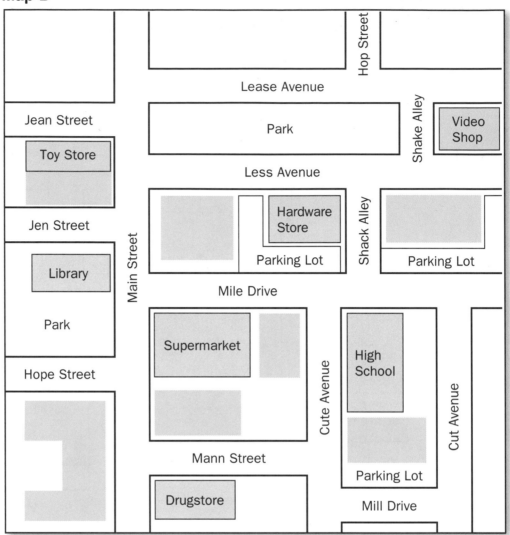

Student B, ask the location of the places in the box.

Places for Map B

bookstore	auto supply store
hospital	preschool
restaurant	bank
post office	

13

Numbers
Checking and correcting mistakes

Did you say "ninety"? No, "nineteen."
What does Shane sell?

A Saying numbers and years

1 Listen. Say each number two times.

1. 30

thirty

13

thirteen

2. 40

forty

14

fourteen

3. 50

fifty

15

fifteen

4. 60
sixty

16
sixteen

2 Listen. Say each year two times.

1. 1999
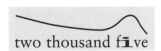
nineteen ninety-nine

3. 2010
two thousand ten

2. 2005
two thousand five

4. 2029
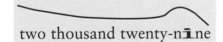
two thousand twenty-nine

Listen. Say each sentence two times.

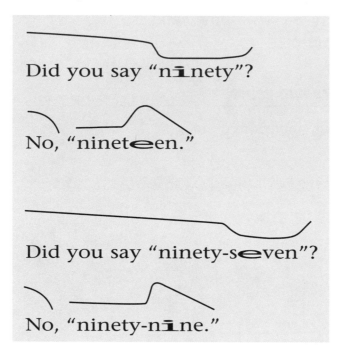

Did you say "ni̱nety"?

No, "ninete͟en."

Did you say "ninety-s͟even"?

No, "ninety-ni̱ne."

C ___ *Pair work: Correcting a mistake about a number* ___

1 Student A, say a number from the Numbers box.

2 Student B, pretend that you did not understand.
Ask about a different number.

3 Student A, correct the mistake.

4 Take turns saying the numbers.

Examples   **Numbers**

Student A: Fifty.
Student B: Did you say "fif**teen**"?
Student A: No, "**fif**ty."
Student B: Twenty-nine.
Student A: Did you say "twenty-**five**"?
Student B: No, "twenty-**nine**."

13	30	16
60	19	90
14	40	17
70	66	67
15	50	18
80	98	99
2018	2080	2020

D Music of English 🎵

Listen. Say the telephone number two times.

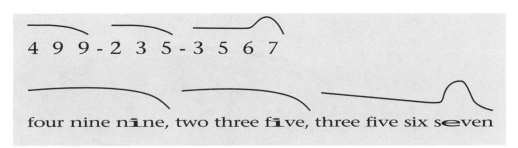

4 9 9 - 2 3 5 - 3 5 6 7

four nine nīne, two three fīve, three five six sɛven

E Listening for pauses in telephone numbers

Telephone numbers are said with a pause (silence)
after each group of numbers. In different countries,
these groups are different.

Listen for the pauses in these telephone numbers.

Australia	03-9568-0322
Canada	604-892-5808
Japan	03-3295-5875
Mexico	55-19-59-39
New Zealand	9-377-3800
United Kingdom	01223-325-847
United States	212-924-3900

F Saying telephone numbers

1 Listen. Say these U.S. telephone numbers two times.
The first two have area codes.

a. 391-456-3304   c. 777-2340

b. 596-415-7892   d. 660-2555

2 Now dictate your own telephone number to a partner.
Check what your partner wrote.

1 Read the Seaside Mall directory below.

2 Listen. Say the name of each store two times.

SEASIDE MALL DIRECTORY

Men	Location	Phone
Mr. True	1A	214-1698
Shane	25B	213-1697

Women	Location	Phone
The Trap	14C	213-2134
Smart Woman	20A	214-1597

Boys	Location	Phone
Red Dog	16A	214-1718

Girls	Location	Phone
Mall Mice	17A	213-1719
California Girl	15A	213-9070

Food	Location	Phone
FastBurger	5B	213-1232
Sunshine Cafe	6C	213-1658
The Elephant Eatery	7B	214-2194

Other Stores	Location	Phone
Small World	15B	215-3200
Gemstones	13B	215-3214
Video Mania	21C	214-5599
Music Universe	31C	214-8790

H Music of English 🎵🎵

Listen. Say each sentence two times.

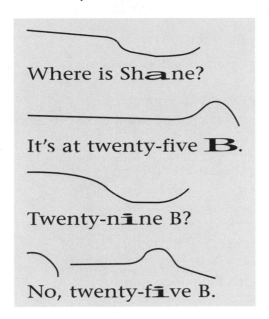

Where is Sh**a**ne?

It's at twenty-five **B**.

Twenty-n**i**ne B?

No, twenty-f**i**ve B.

I Pair work: Calling for information

1 There are three levels at the Seaside Mall:
Level A, B, and C. Listen to this phone conversation.

2 Say the conversation two times with a partner.

Clerk: Seaside Mall. May I help you?
Customer: Yes, please. What's the telephone number for the Sunshine Cafe?
Clerk: 213-1658.
Customer: 213-1698?
Clerk: No, 213-1658.
Customer: Okay. Where is it?
Clerk: It's at 6C.
Customer: Thanks.
Clerk: You're welcome.

Pair work: Where is it? What's the telephone number?

1 Customer, look at the Places box below. (Don't look at the Seaside Mall directory.) Ask for the location and telephone number of a store.

2 Clerk, look at the directory on page 94. Answer.

3 Customer, check your answer with your partner. Then write the location and telephone number in the box.

4 Take turns as the customer and clerk at the information desk.

Example

Customer:	Excuse me, where is The Trap?
Clerk:	It's at 14C.
Customer:	Thanks. What's the phone number?
Clerk:	It's 213-2134.
Customer:	213-2134?
Clerk:	That's right.

Places

	Location	Phone
Mr. True	....	....
Shane	....	....
The Trap	....	....
Smart Woman	....	....
Red Dog	....	....
Mall Mice	....	....
California Girl	....	....
FastBurger	....	....
Sunshine Cafe	....	....
The Elephant Eatery	....	....
Small World	....	....
Gemstones	....	....
Video Mania	....	....
Music Universe	....	....

Listen to information about the stores at the Seaside Mall.

SEASIDE MALL

	$$$ Expensive	$$ Moderate $ Inexpensive
$$$	The Trap	clothes for women
$	Mr. True	clothes for men
$$	Shane	clothes for men
$	Smart Woman	clothes for women
$$	Small World	toys
$$$	Gemstones	jewelry
$$	Music Universe	music CDs and tapes
$$	Video Mania	videos and video games
$$	Mall Mice	clothes for girls
$$$	California Girl	clothes for girls
$	Red Dog	clothes for boys
$$$	Sunshine Cafe	big sandwiches
$$	The Elephant Eatery	soup, salad, and pizza
$	FastBurger	burgers and ice cream

🎧 **L** ___Music of English___ 🎵🎶

Listen. Say each sentence two times.

What does Shane sell?

Clothes for men.

Did you say clothes for teens?

No, for men.

M Pair work: Checking information

1 Listen to the conversation.

2 Say the conversation two times with a partner.

Customer: What does Smart Woman sell?
　Clerk: Clothes for women.
Customer: Did you say clothes for **teens**?
　Clerk: No, for **women**.
Customer: Is it expensive?
　Clerk: No. It's **in**expensive.
Customer: Thanks.
　Clerk: You're very welcome.

3 Take turns as the customer and the clerk. Ask what a store sells and if it is expensive. Find the answers in the box in K, page 97.

N More linking

Listen. Say each sentence two times.

1. Continuing sound + vowel sound

   Smart Woman is inexpensive.　　　Smart　Womannnizzzinexpensive　.

   FastBurger opens at ten.　　　FastBurgerrropenzzzat　ten.

2. Stop sound + vowel sound

   The Trap is closed on Sundays.　　The　Trapis closedon　Sundays.

   Small World is fun.　　　Small　Worldis　fun.

3. Continuing sound + continuing sound

   FastBurger never costs much.　　FastBurgerrrnever　costs much.

   Teens like shopping.　　　Teenzzzlike　shopping.

4. Vowel sound + vowel sound

   Mr. True is inexpensive.　　　Mr.　Trueuuizzz　inexpensive.

   Video Mania is busy.　　　Video　Maniaaais　busy.

5. Same sound to same sound

   Gemstones sells jewelry.　　　Gemstonessssells　jewelry.

   John never buys books.　　　Johnnnnever　buys books.

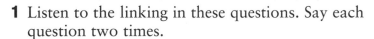

O Linking with vowels

1 Listen to the linking in these questions. Say each question two times.

2 Draw lines to link vowel sounds.

1. Are you in the movies?
2. Are you alive?
3. Are you an actor?
4. Are you on TV?
5. Did you ever play sports?
6. Who are you?

P Twenty Questions game   EXTRA

Play this game with your class. Student A is a famous person. (For example, a movie star, singer, politician, or artist.) Take turns asking yes/no questions until someone guesses who Student A is. The goal is to guess who the person is in fewer than twenty questions.

Example

Student A: (You decide to be Elvis Presley.)
Student B: Are you alive?
Student A: No.
Student C: Are you a man?
Student A: Yes.

(Questions continue.)

Here are some example questions. Make up your own questions, too.

1. Are you alive?
2. Are you a man?
3. Are you an actor?
4. Are you an artist?
5. Are you a politician?
6. Do we buy your records?
7. Do we hear you on the radio?
8. Do we see you on TV?
9. Are you in the movies?
10. Were you in *Star Wars*?

14

Final sounds N, L, ND, and LD
Linking with N, L, ND, and LD

What's a trail? A path.

A   Final sounds N, L, and D

Look at these pictures.

L	N	D

Looking to the side

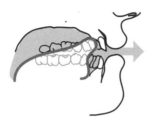 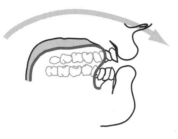 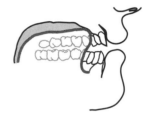

Air continues out of the mouth	Air continues out of the nose only	Air stops

Looking to the front

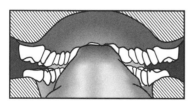  

bellll   Bennn   bed

Air continues	Air continues	Air stops

🎧 **B** *Listening for final sounds N and L*

Listen to the final sound of each word. Do not say the words.

1. mine   mile
2. nine   Nile
3. can   call
4. ten   tell
5. man   mall
6. win   will
7. pin   pill
8. when   well

🎧 **C** *Which word is different?*

1 Listen. Mark the different word.

	X	Y	Z	
1.		✔		(ten, tell, ten)
2.				
3.				
4.				
5.				
6.				
7.				
8.				

2 Listen again.

🎧 **D** *Which word do you hear?*

1 Listen. Circle the word you hear.

1. (bone)   bowl   (bone)
2. rain   rail
3. main   mail
4. when   well
5. fine   file
6. pain   pail
7. train   trail
8. ten   tell

2 Listen again.

E Saying final sounds N and L

Listen. Say each word two times.

1.	pin	pill	6.	main	mail
2.	win	will	7.	cone	coal
3.	bone	bowl	8.	when	well
4.	rain	rail	9.	then	they'll
5.	can	call	10.	train	trail

F Saying final sounds ND and LD

Listen. Say each word two times.

1.	find	filed
2.	phoned	fold
3.	trained	trailed
4.	mind	mild
5.	spend	spelled
6.	owned	old

G Music of English 🎵🎶

Listen. Say each sentence two times. Be careful with the final sounds in the most important words.

What's a trail?

A thing to ride in.

No, what's a trail?

A path.

Right.

H *Pair work: What's a train for?*

1 Student A, ask question **a** or **b**.

2 Student B, answer.

3 Student A, if the answer is correct, say "Right." If it is wrong, ask again.

4 Take turns asking questions.

Example

> Student A: What's a train for?
> Student B: To walk on.
> Student A: No, what's a **train** for?
> Student B: To ride in.
> Student A: Right.

1. a. What's a trail for?   To walk on.
   b. What's a train for?   To ride in.

2. a. What's a trail?   A path.
   b. What's a train?   A thing to ride in.

3. a. How do you spell "trail"?   T - R - A - I - L.
   b. How do you spell "train"?   T - R - A - I - N.

4. a. What's a pin?   A sharp thing.
   b. What's a pill?   Medicine.

5. a. What's a pin for?   To stick things together.
   b. What's a pill for?   To help a sick person.

6. a. How do you spell "main"?   M - A - I - N.
   b. How do you spell "mail"?   M - A - I - L.

7. a. How do you spell "fold"?   F - O - L - D.
   b. How do you spell "phoned"? P - H - O - N - E - D.

8. a. What does "fold" mean?   To put one part on
                                     top of another part.
   b. What does "phoned" mean?   The past of "phone."

9. a. How do you spell "owned"?   O - W - N - E - D.
   b. How do you spell "old"?   O - L - D.

I Linking with L, N, LD, and ND

1 Listen. Say these words two times.

Call our friends.	Callllour friends.
Hold on.	Holdon .
Spend it.	Spendit .
phone number	phonennnumber

2 Listen. Say each sentence two times.

1. We call our friends. — We callllour friends.
2. We called our boss. — We calledour boss.
3. Hold on tight. — Holdon tight.
4. They can always go. — They cannnalways go.
5. When are you coming? — Whennnare you coming?
6. Don't spend all the money. — Don't spendall the money.
7. She spelled every word right. — She spelledevery word right.
8. What's your phone number? — What's your phonennnumber ?

J Pair work: Checking information

1 Listen to the conversations.

2 Say the conversations with a partner.

1. The Emergency

   Aunt: The baby swallowed a pill!
   Mother: A pin! Call the doctor!
   Aunt: Not a **pin**, a **pill**.
   Mother: Pin or pill, we have to call the doctor!

2. In a Downtown Office Building

   Visitor: Excuse me, where's the main office?
   Clerk: The main office? Do you mean where you can get information?
   Visitor: No, I mean where I can buy stamps.
   Clerk: Oh, you mean "**mail**"!
   Visitor: Yes, the mail office.
   Clerk: Actually, it's called the **post** office. It's in the next building to the right, and there's a mailbox in front of it.

3. The Misunderstanding

Father: Did you fold them?
    Son: Fold what?
Father: The shirts I left for you to fold.
    Son: Did you say **"fold them"**? I thought you said **"Phone Tim."**
Father: Did you phone Tim?
    Son: Yes! I told him you left some shirts. He thought it was strange!

K *The mirror test: Final sounds N and L* EXTRA

1 Find a small mirror and follow these steps.

1. Hold the mirror close to your face, under your nose.

2. Say the sound **N** strongly.

3. Quickly look at the mirror. You should see a cloud.

Nnnnn

4. Say the word "bone." You should see a cloud again.

5. Say the sound **L** strongly. You should not see a cloud.

Lllll

6. Say the word "bowl." You should not see a cloud.

2 Try the mirror test with the words below. Check your mirror after each word.

cone   coal
seen   seal
ten   tell
can   call
pin   pill

15

Final sounds S, TH, and T
Linking with TH

What's a bath for? To get clean.

🎧 A Final sounds S, TH, and T

1 Look at these pictures.

S   TH   T

Looking to the front

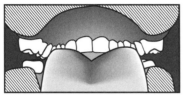   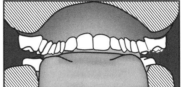   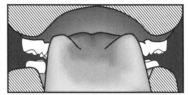

Looking down

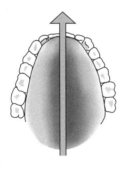   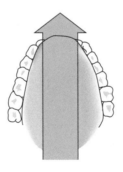   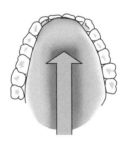

mass   math   mat

Air continues   Air continues   Air stops

2 Listen for the sound at the end of these words.
Do not say the words.

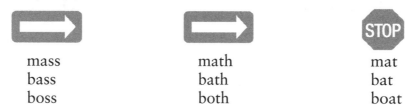

mass	math	mat
bass	bath	bat
boss	both	boat

B Which word is different?

1 Listen. Mark the different word.

	X	Y	Z	
1.	....	✔	....	(boat, both, boat)
2.	....	....	....	
3.	....	....	....	
4.	....	....	....	
5.	....	....	....	
6.	....	....	....	
7.	....	....	....	
8.	....	....	....	

2 Listen again.

C Which word do you hear?

1 Listen. Circle the word you hear.

1.	both	boat	(both)
2.	path	pat	
3.	mass	mat	
4.	fourth	fort	
5.	force	fort	
6.	nice	night	
7.	rice	right	
8.	face	fate	
9.	with	wit	
10.	race	rate	

2 Listen again.

D Saying final TH

1 Look again at the picture of how to say **TH**.

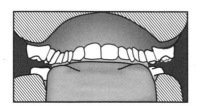

2 Listen. Say each word two times.

1. bath
2. both
3. teeth
4. math
5. mouth

E Saying final TH and T/D in numbers

Listen. Say each number two times.

1. first — first
2. second — second
3. third — third
4. fourth — fourththth
5. fifth — fifththth
6. sixth — sixththth
7. seventh — seventhththth
8. eighth — eighththth
9. ninth — nineththth
10. tenth — tenththth

F Saying final sounds S/Z, TH, and T

Listen. Say each word two times.

S/Z	TH	T
1. bass	bath	bat
bassss	baththth	bat
2. mass	math	mat
massss	maththth	mat
3. boss	both	boat
bossss	boththth	boat
4. fours	fourth	fort
fourzzz	fourththth	fort

G Music of English 🎵

Listen. Say each sentence two times.

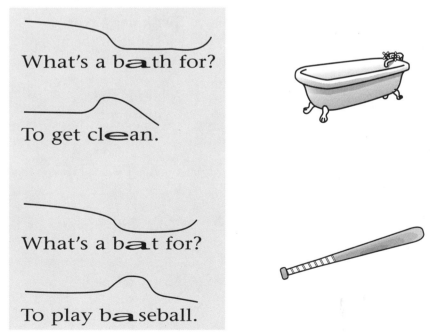

What's a b**a**th for?

To get cl**ea**n.

What's a b**a**t for?

To play b**a**seball.

H Pair work: What's a bath for?

1 Student A, ask question **a** or **b**.

2 Student B, answer.

3 Student A, if the answer is correct, say "Right." If it is wrong, ask again.

4 Take turns asking questions.

Examples

Student A: How do you spell "bat"?
Student B: B - A - T - H.
Student A: No. How do you spell "bat"?

Student B: What's a bath for?
Student A: To get clean.
Student B: Right.

1. a. How do you spell "bath"?   B - A - T - H.
   b. How do you spell "bat"?   B - A - T.

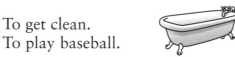

2. a. What's a bath for?   To get clean.
   b. What's a bat for?   To play baseball.

3. a. What does "both" mean?   Two things. Not
                                   just one of them.
   b. What does "boat" mean?   A small ship.

4. a. What does "bath" mean?   A tub, in the
                                   bathroom.
   b. What does "bass" mean?   A kind of fish.

5. a. How do you spell "faith"?   F - A - I - T - H.
   b. How do you spell "face"?   F - A - C - E.

6. a. What does "math" mean?   Work with numbers.
   b. What does "mat" mean?   A small rug.

7. a. How do you spell "math"?   M - A - T - H.
   b. How do you spell "mass"?   M - A - S - S.

8. a. What does "mouse" mean?   A small animal.
   b. What does "mouth" mean?   It's used for eating
                                   and speaking.

9. a. What comes after "night"? Day.
   b. What comes after "ninth"? Tenth.

10. a. What's a path?   A small trail.
    b. What's a pass?   A free ticket.

I Pair work: Checking days and dates

1 Student A, say a day, month, and date from the box.

2 Student B, check what your partner said.

3 Student A, if the answer is correct, say "Right."
If it is wrong, give the correct answer.

4 Take turns saying the days and dates.

Examples

Student A: Tuesday, March first.
Student B: Did you say "Thursday"?
Student A: No, **"Tuesday."**
Student B: Monday, April fourth.
Student A: Did you say "April fifth"?
Student B: No, "April **fourth**."

Day	Month	Date
Monday	January	first
Tuesday	February	second
Wednesday	March	third
Thursday	April	fourth
Friday	May	fifth
Saturday	June	sixth
Sunday	July	seventh
	August	eighth
	September	ninth
	October	tenth
	November	
	December	

J   Linking with TH

1 Listen to these groups of words.

both of them   boththth of   them

Fourth of July   Fourthththof   July

math and English   maththth and   English

both things   boththth things

2 Listen. Say each sentence two times.

1. I want a bath after
   dinner.   I want a baththth after dinner.

2. It was the Fourth of
   July.   It was the Fourthththof July.

3. Both of them came.   Boththth of them came.

4. Sue is studying
   math and English.   Sue is studying maththth and English.

5. Her teeth are
   very white.   Her teethththare very white.

6. The path over the
   mountain is hard.   The paththth over the mountain is hard.

7. The path through
   the woods is easy.   The paththth through the woods is easy.

8. We both think you
   should come.   We boththth think you should come.

9. They both thank
   you.   They boththth thank you.

10. He left both things
    at home.   He left boththth things at home.

K   Review: Linking

Listen. Say each sentence two times.

1. Continuing sound + vowel sound

   When is the store open?   Whennn is the storerr open ?

   Will it open before eight?   Willll it open beforerr eight ?

112 • Unit 15

2. Stop sound + vowel sound

The bank opens at eight.   The bankopens ateight .

I'd like a cup of tea.   I'd likea cupof tea.

3. Continuing sound + continuing sound

She wants fish.   She wantsssfish .

The store's near Main.   The storezzznearrrMain .

4. Vowel sound + vowel sound.

Does he ever drink   Does hcccever drink coffeeeeor tea?
   coffee or tea?

Make the dog go away.   Make the dog goooaway .

She adores vanilla ice   Sheeeadores vanillaaaice cream.
   cream.

5. Same sound + same sound

Will Lucy arrive soon?   WillllLucy arrive soon?

Please stop pushing!   Pleasezzstoppushing !

6. Linking a group of words

Go away! Far away!   Goooaway! Farrraway !

Come again whenever you   Comemmagain wheneverrryou wantto .
   want to.

Will it open at ten?   Willllitopennnatttten ?

Will it open before nine?   Willllitopen beforerrnine ?

Bob ate all of the fish soup.   Bobatealllof the fishshshsoup .

16 Review

🎧 **A** _Counting syllables: The Sunshine Cafe_ ☐ ☐ ☐

1 Listen to the menu for the Sunshine Cafe.

Sunshine Cafe

The world's most spectacular sandwiches! A mile high!

These sandwiches are an adventure!

The San Francisco

Fish, avocado, lettuce, tomatoes, and artichoke

The Honolulu

Baked chicken, pineapple, red onions, and mayonnaise

The Toronto

Smoked chicken, roasted bell peppers, and cream cheese

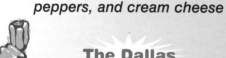

The Dallas

Barbecued beef, hot peppers, and onions

The New York

Corned beef, pickles, tomatoes, and mustard

The L.A.

Cheese, sun-dried tomatoes, cucumbers, and butter

PLAIN SANDWICHES

Peanut butter and jelly
Tuna salad
Egg salad

Choice of bread:
white, whole wheat, rye, French roll

 BEVERAGES

Coffee, tea, iced tea, milk, lemonade, Coke, sparkling water

2 Write the answers to these questions.

1. Write the name of one of the sandwiches. ....
2. How many syllables are in the name of this sandwich? ....
3. How many syllables are in the first food in the sandwich? ....
4. Which beverage has the most syllables? ....
5. How many syllables does it have? ....

3 Listen to the menu again. Check your answers.

Write one word from the menu in each box in the chart.
You can use the same word in two boxes.

	One syllable	Two syllables	Three syllables
Two Vowel Rule Circle the alphabet vowel.	b(a)k e d	r(o)a s t e d	a r t i c h(o)k e
One Vowel Rule Circle the relative vowel.	f(i)s h	p(e)p p e r s	l(e)m o n a d e
Strong syllables Circle the strong syllable.		(pep)p e r s	(sand)w i c h e s
Final stop sounds Circle the final stop sound.	h o(t)	m u s t a r(d)	a r t i c h o(k)e
Final continuing sounds Circle the final continuing sound.	b e l(l)	c h i c k e(n)	m a y o n n a i(s)e

Listen. Say the conversation two times.

I'd like the Toronto, please.

The Toronto?

Yes, on white.

Okay, on white.

No, I changed my mind. On whole wheat.

Okay. One Toronto, on whole wheat.

🎧 **D** *Pair work: The most important word*

1 Listen to these conversations. Circle the most important word in each sentence.

2 Say the conversations with a partner. Take turns as the customer and the server.

1. Customer: I'd like the Toronto, please.
      Server: The Toronto?
    Customer: Yes, on whole wheat.
      Server: Okay. One Toronto, on whole wheat.
                 Coming right up!

2. Customer: I'd like the Honolulu, please.
     Server: Okay, one Honolulu. What kind of bread?
   Customer: Whole wheat. No, I changed my mind.
             I'd like the San Francisco.
     Server: One San Francisco. On a French roll?
   Customer: That sounds good.
     Server: And to drink?
   Customer: Tea.
     Server: Hot tea?
   Customer: No, iced tea.
     Server: Thank you.

E   *Pair work: Finding the most important word*

1 Read these conversations. Discuss with your partner which words are most important. Circle the most important words.

2 Take turns as the customer and the server.

   1. The Happy Customer

      Customer: What's the best sandwich?
        Server: The Honolulu.
      Customer: Is that the one with
                pineapple?
        Server: Yes. And chicken.
      Customer: Smoked chicken?
        Server: No, baked chicken.
      Customer: That sounds fine!

   2. The Difficult Server

      Customer: I'd like the San Francisco, please.
        Server: No fish today.
      Customer: Well, then I'd like the Toronto.
        Server: No chicken today.
      Customer: Do you have anything?
        Server: Cheese. But the cheese is bad.
      Customer: Then just bring me coffee.

3. The Difficult Customer

Customer: Bring me a Toronto.
  Server: That's with chicken.
Customer: No, I want beef.
  Server: The Dallas has beef.
Customer: Barbecued beef?
  Server: Yes.
Customer: Oh, no! I hate barbecued beef! I'll have the one with fish.
  Server: Okay, one San Francisco. And to drink?
Customer: Coffee. But it has to be hot. Really hot.
  Server: Okay. Whatever will make you happy.

F Music of English

Listen. Say this conversation two times.

I'd like the Dallas, please.

One Dallas. On rye?

Yes, but with bell peppers.

Not hot peppers?

No, bell peppers. Roasted bell peppers.

Okay. One Dallas, on rye, with bell peppers.

G Pair work: Ordering at the Sunshine Cafe

1 Work with a partner. Take turns as the customer and the server.

2 Customer, order a sandwich from the menu on page 114.

3 Server, check to make sure you understood.

4 Customer, say Yes, correct an error, or change your mind.

H Check yourself: Syllables, linking, and most important words

1 Record yourself saying the conversation. Say both parts,
X and Y. (If you do not have a tape recorder, ask a
partner to listen.)

The Beach

Line
1 X: We rented a car.
2 Y: You painted a car?
3 X: No, we rented a car.
4   We went to the beach.
5 Y: When did you go?
6 X: Wednesday.
7 Y: But it was raining!
8 X: That's okay. When we
9   plan a trip, we go!

2 Listen to your tape three times. Each time, complete
a checklist below. (If you are working with a partner, say the
conversation three times, one for each checklist. Your partner
can complete the checklists.)

Checklist 1: Syllables
Did you get the right number of syllables in these words?

Line		Yes	No	
1	rented	....	....	(2)
2	painted	....	....	(2)
6	Wednesday	....	....	(2)
7	raining	....	....	(2)
9	plan	....	....	(1)

Checklist 2: Linking
Did you link these words?

Line		Yes	No	
1	rented a	....	....	renteda
2	painted a	....	....	painteda
4	went to	....	....	wentto
7	was raining	....	....	wazzzraining
8	That's okay	....	....	Thatsssokay
9	plan a	....	....	plannna

Checklist 3: Most important words
Did your voice go up or down on these words?

Line		Yes	No	
1	car	....	....	car
2	painted	....	....	painted
3	rented	....	....	rented
4	beach	....	....	beach
5	go	....	....	go
6	Wednesday	....	....	Wednesday
7	raining	....	....	raining
9	plan	....	....	plan
9	go	....	....	go

3 Record the conversation again. (Or, say it again for your partner.) Listen for your improvement.

I *Check yourself: Final sounds, linking, and most important words*

1 Record yourself saying the conversation. Say both parts, **X** and **Y**. (If you do not have a tape recorder, ask a partner to listen.)

A Party

Line
1 X: We're having a party tomorrow night.
2 Y: What kind of party?
3 X: A birthday party.
4 Y: Who's it for?
5 X: My sister. She's going to be nineteen.
6 Y: Who's coming?
7 X: A lot of people.

Line
8   Y: Are all your relatives coming?
9   X: Yes, everybody but Aunt Ann. She's not well.
10   Y: Oh, that's too bad.

2 Listen to your tape three times. Each time, complete a checklist below. (If you are working with a partner, say the conversation three times, one for each checklist. Your partner can complete the checklists.)

Checklist 1: Final sounds
Did you say the final sounds clearly in these words?

Line		Yes	No	
1	We're	....	....	➡
2	kind	....	....	STOP
4	Who's	....	....	➡
5	sister	....	....	➡
5	nineteen	....	....	➡
7	lot	....	....	STOP
8	relatives	....	....	➡
9	Aunt	....	....	STOP
10	bad	....	....	STOP

Checklist 2: Linking
Did you link these words?

Line		Yes	No	
2	kind of	....	....	kindof
4	Who's it	....	....	Whozzzit
7	lot of	....	....	lotof
8	Are all	....	....	Arerrall
8	your relatives	....	....	yourrrrelatives
9	She's not	....	....	Shezzznot

Checklist 3: Most important words
Did your voice go up or down on these words?

Line		Yes	No	
1	party	....	....	party
2	kind	....	....	kind
3	birthday	....	....	birthday
4	for	....	....	for
5	sister	....	....	sister
5	nineteen	....	....	nineteen
6	coming	....	....	coming
7	lot	....	....	lot
8	relatives	....	....	relatives
9	Ann	....	....	Ann
9	well	....	....	well
10	bad	....	....	bad

3 Record the conversation again. (Or, say it again for your partner.) Listen for your improvement.

J   Review: Syllables, linking, and most important words

1 Record yourself saying this conversation the same way you did before.

A Trip in the U.S.A.

Line
1   X: I'm planning a trip.
2   Y: A long trip?
3   X: No, just a short one.
4   Y: Where are you going?
5   X: Washington.
6   Y: The capital?
7   X: No, Washington State.
8   Y: That's a long trip!
9   X: Oh, we're flying. So it won't take long.
10 Y: Is this for business?
11 X: No, just for a vacation.
12 Y: Well, have a super trip!

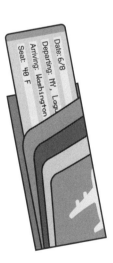

2 Listen to your tape three times. Each time, complete a checklist below.

Checklist 1: Syllables
Did you say the right number of syllables in these words?

Line		Yes	No	
1	planning	....	....	(2)
5	Washington	....	....	(3)
6	capital	....	....	(3)
9	flying	....	....	(2)
10	business	....	....	(2)
11	vacation	....	....	(3)
12	super	....	....	(2)

Checklist 2: Linking
Did you link these words?

Line		Yes	No	
3	just a	....	....	justa
4	Where are you	....	....	Whererrarerryou
8	That's a	....	....	Thatsssa
11	for a	....	....	forrra
12	have a	....	....	havevva

Checklist 3: Most important word
Did your voice go up or down on these words?

Line		Yes	No	
1	trip	....	....	trip
2	long	....	....	long
3	short	....	....	short
4	going	....	....	going
5	Washington	....	....	Washington
6	capital	....	....	capital
7	state	....	....	state
8	long	....	....	long
9	flying	....	....	flying
9	won't	....	....	won't
10	business	....	....	business
11	vacation	....	....	vacation
12	super	....	....	super

---

3 Now record the conversation again. Listen for how you have improved.

Appendix A
Parts of the mouth

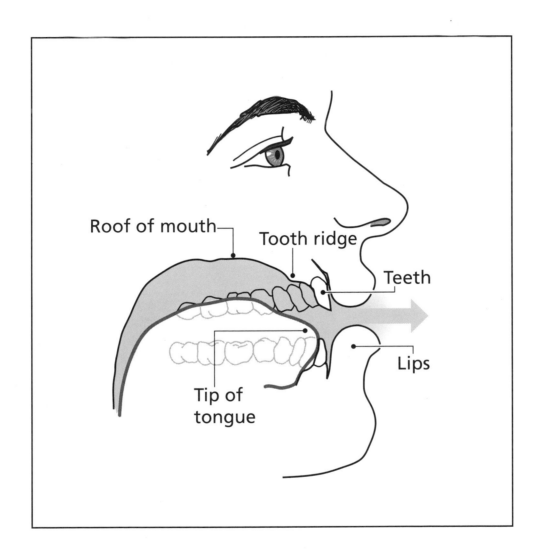

Appendix B

Tongue shape for T/D, S/Z, L, R, and TH

The photographs on the left show wax models. They are not real mouths.

Looking to the front

T/D

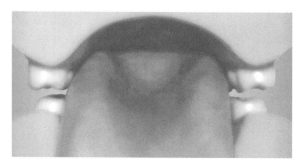

S/Z

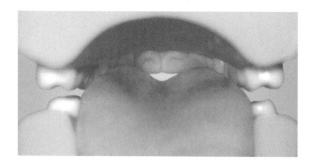
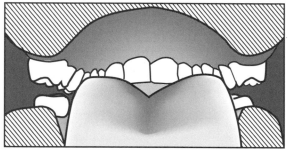

L

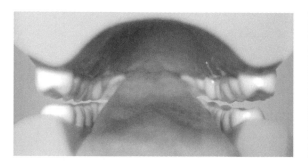
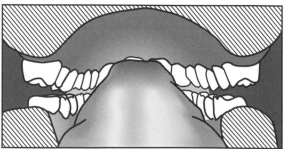

Looking to the front

R

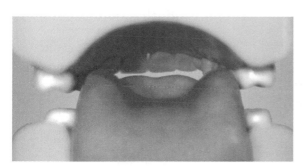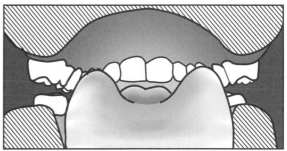

TH

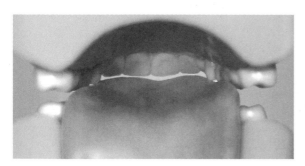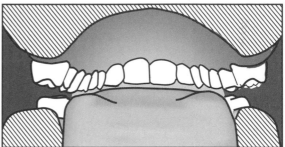

Appendix C

Vowels A^y, I^y, and U^w

Looking from the side   How the mouth moves

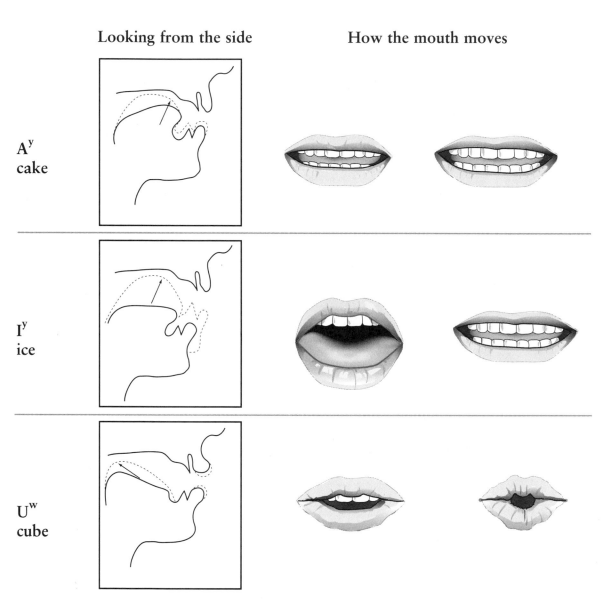

A^y
cake

I^y
ice

U^w
cube

Note: This line (-----) shows where
the tongue, teeth, and lips END.

Appendix D
Vowel rules

A Review of Vowel Rules

These rules work for many words.

The Two Vowel Rule

When there are two vowel letters in a syllable:

1. The first vowel says its alphabet name.
2. The second vowel is silent.

A^y	E^y	I^y	O^w	U^w
cake	tea	ice	cone	cube
remain	repeat	arrive	soapy	excuse

The One Vowel Rule

When there is only one vowel letter in a syllable:

1. The vowel letter does NOT say its alphabet name.
2. The vowel letter says its RELATIVE sound.

A	E	I	O	U
can	pencil	finger	hot	summer
Mack	Jenny	Kitty	John	Russ

B The letters -y and -w as vowels

1 The letter -y sometimes sounds like E^y.

E^y
city	history	liberty
pretty	bakery	lottery
silly	electricity	comedy
company	jewelry	

2 The letter -y sometimes sounds like I^y.

I^y
sky	fly	apply
why	my	type
try		

3 Sometimes the letters -y and -w act like a second vowel when they follow the letter -a- or -o-. Then the word may follow the Two Vowel Rule.

A^y
pay	stay	way
say	tray	today
play	may	yesterday
day	gray	

O^w
show	below	snow
slow	throw	rainbow
grow	arrow	pillow
bowl	low	know

C More words that follow the vowel rules

1 Word pairs

A^y	A	E^y	E	I^y	I	O^w	O	U^w	U
ate	at	read	red	mile	mill	coat	cot	suit	sun
rain	ran	seat	set	file	fill	clothes	cloth	true	run
make	Mac	seal	sell	type	tip	soak	sock	blue	bun
same	Sam	mean	men	time	Tim	note	not	tube	tub
rate	rat	beat	bet	style	still	hope	hop	cue	cup

2 The Two Vowel Rule

There are two vowel letters in the FIRST syllable of these words.

A^y	E^y	I^y	O^w	U^w
painting	freeway	Iceland	floating	Tuesday
sailboat	seated	pineapple	soapy	useful

There are two vowel letters in the LAST syllable of these words.

A^y	E^y	I^y	O^w	U^w
erase	delete	inside	alone	introduce
female	asleep	alive	compose	assume
explain	retreat	define	grown	produce
delay	esteem	provide	revoke	accuse
became	reveal	arise	awoke	include
parade	supreme	replied	window	continue

3 The One Vowel Rule

There is one vowel letter in the FIRST syllable of these words.

A	E	I	O	U
after	enter	history	cotton	ugly
master	yellow	mister	problem	running
planning	fellow	missing	copy	Sunday
asking	effort	spilling	hotter	under
practice	tennis	Internet	omelet	thunder
manner	television	children	comma	supper
Saturday	relative	window	stopping	

There is one vowel letter in the LAST syllable of these words.

A	E	I	O	U
attach	pretend	forbid	mailbox	unplug
subtract	suggest	politics	adopt	instruct
expand	protest	begin	workshop	product
contract	forget	morning	apricot	begun

Appendix E

How often do the vowel rules work?

A The Two Vowel Rule

> When there are two vowel letters in a syllable:
> 1. The first vowel says its alphabet name.
> 2. The second vowel is silent.
>
> cake   tea   ice   cone   cube

This rule works for many words, but not all. The chart below shows how often the Two Vowel Rule works. For example, the letters -ai- have the A^y sound 95% of the time.

How often does the Two Vowel Rule work?			
Letters	**Sounds**	**Percent of time***	**Examples**
-ai- -a- + final -e -ay	A^y	95% 89% 93%	rain, train, afraid cake, came, ate day, say, play
-e at the end of words -e- + final -e -ee- and -ea- -y	E^y	82% 32% most of the time† 95%	he, me, she Pete, athlete tree, tea, please city, money, lucky
-i- + final -e -igh	I^y	80% 100%	ice, time, fine high, night, light
-o- + final -e	O^w	76%	home, phone, alone
-u- + final -e -oo-	U^w	94% 88%	cute, accuse, flute room, choose, school

* Source: *A Survey of English Spelling*, Edward Carney, Routledge, London, 1994. These numbers refer to the percentage of times that this spelling produces this vowel sound, based on analyses of multisyllabic words.

† No figure given.

B   *The One Vowel Rule*

> When there is only one vowel letter in a syllable:
> 1. The vowel letter does NOT say its alphabet name.
> 2. The vowel letter says its RELATIVE sound.
>
> can   pencil   finger   hot   summer

This rule works for many words, but not all. The chart below shows how often the One Vowel Rule works. For example, the letter -a- has the sound **A** 91% of the time.

How often does the One Vowel Rule work?			
Letter	Sounds	Percent of time*	Examples
a	A	91%	has, cat, aspirin, answer
e	E	82%	bed, message, medicine
i	I	93%	his, big, simple, children
o	O	74%	stop, shop, problem
u	U	66%	up, sun, butter, hundred

* Source: *A Survey of English Spelling*, Edward Carney, Routledge, London, 1994. These numbers refer to the percentage of times that this spelling produces this vowel sound, based on analyses of multisyllabic words.